Essential Elements for Choir

TEACHER RESOURCE KIT

Developed by

New York, New York   Columbus, Ohio   Woodland Hills, California   Peoria, Illinois

SENIOR AUTHOR
Dr. Janice Killian, Music Education
Texas Woman's University, Denton, Texas

AUTHOR
Debbie Helm Daniel, Choral Director
Formerly of Garland Independent School District, Texas

AUTHOR
Linda Rann, Product Manager
Essential Elements
Hal Leonard Corporation, Milwaukee, Wisconsin

Glencoe/McGraw-Hill

*A Division of The **McGraw-Hill** Companies*

Printed in the United States of America.

Send all inquiries to:
Glencoe/McGraw Hill
21600 Oxnard Street, Suite 500
Woodland Hills, CA 91367

ISBN 0-07-826063-9

2 3 4 5 6 7 8 9 045 07 06 05 04 03 02 01

CONTENTS

Page

LISTING OF TITLES

INTRODUCTION

The *Teacher Resource Kit* is a valuable teaching aid for the busy choral director. This book contains over 120 reproducible student activity pages on the subjects of voice development, music theory, melodic and rhythmic reading, rehearsal and performance techniques, concert etiquette, music listening, music history, and music activities linked to other subject areas in the curriculum. Assessment tools are provided in the form of charts, checklists, quizzes, writing activities, listening lessons and more. The enclosed Listening CD includes recordings designed for use with many of the lessons.

For the teacher are lesson plans for each student activity sheet. These teacher lessons include lesson objectives, an explanation of the activity, a suggestion for teaching the activity and answers to all questions.

Use the *Teacher Resource Kit*

- On a regular basis to assess student progress.
- With the Listening CD to teach the major eras in music history.
- For additional practice pages for the slow learner or new student to choir.
- As enrichment activities for the advanced student.
- To provide prepared materials for use by the substitute teacher.

Note: Permission has been granted to reproduce student activity pages only. This permission is limited to the purchaser of the book for use in one school.

MUSICIANSHIP

- **Voice Builders**
- **Theory Builders**
- **Sight-Reading Melodic Assessment**
- **Sight-Reading Rhythmic Assessment**

POSTURE

NAME ____________________

DATE ____________________

Directions: Stand in excellent singing position. Evaluate yourself (from video tape) or ask a partner to evaluate your posture. Identify which areas need improvement. Repeat this evaluation frequently.

_____1. Feet apart; weight on both feet

_____2. Knees unlocked

_____3. Back straight; spinal column lengthened

_____4. Head erect, aligned with your spine

_____5. Rib cage lifted

_____6. Shoulders relaxed

_____7. Hands at your side

Now fold this paper in half so you are unable to see the top portion. In the space provided below, list the seven points of good posture. Try to list them in the order in which they appear on this page.

1. ____________________

2. ____________________

3. ____________________

4. ____________________

5. ____________________

6. ____________________

7. ____________________

BREATHING

NAME ______________________________

DATE ______________________________

Directions: Inhale and then sing a long tone on a comfortable pitch. Evaluate yourself (from video tape) or ask a partner to evaluate your breathing techniques. Identify which areas need improvement. Repeat this evaluation frequently.

_____ Inhaled with a full, deep breath

_____ Kept shoulders steady and relaxed; shoulders should not move during inhalation

_____ Rib cage remained lifted; upper chest should not move during inhalation

_____ Expanded slightly at the waistline while inhaling

_____ Avoided sucking in the stomach while inhaling

FURTHER BREATHING ACTIVITIES TO TRY ON YOUR OWN

ACTIVITY #1

Lie on your back on the floor and concentrate on your breathing process. Where is there movement? in the shoulders? the stomach? the chest? Now stand and try to maintain or imitate the floor breathing techniques while in a standing position. Repeat this activity until you can successfully imitate the floor breathing techniques while standing.

ACTIVITY #2

Stand and gently place your hands above your belt with fingertips touching. Inhale. As you inhale, your muscles should force your fingertips slightly apart, indicating an expansion of your body as you inhale. Shoulders should remain down and relaxed. Keep practicing this exercise until you can do it correctly.

VOWELS

NAME ____________________

DATE ____________________

VOWEL CHECKLIST

I need improvement in the areas checked below. I need to pay special attention to the specific vowels circled.

1. _____ Relax and drop jaw more

   ee eh ah oh oo All

2. _____ Sing with taller vowels (Pull in the corners of the mouth.)

   ee eh ah oh oo All

3. _____ Sing with more space inside the mouth

   ee eh ah oh oo All

4. _____ My vowels were sung correctly with a relaxed jaw, a vertical mouth shape, and with space inside my mouth.

USE THIS CHECKLIST IN THREE DIFFERENT WAYS:

- Sing a familiar song. Evaluate how well you were able to sing the song using correct vowels by completing the checklist above.
- Ask someone to videotape you singing a familiar song. After viewing the video, evaluate how well you were able to sing using correct vowels. Complete checklist again.
- Discuss differences between your original self-evaluation and what you observed after watching the video. What did you learn about yourself as a singer doing this exercise?

Evaluate your vowels frequently throughout the year using this checklist.

DIPHTHONGS

NAME ______________________________

DATE ______________________________

A diphthong (dif-thong) is a combination of two vowel sounds: the primary vowel sound and the secondary vowel sound. The secondary vowel sound is (usually) at the very end of the diphthong, just before the final consonant or next word or syllable. This worksheet will help you become aware of the components of diphthongs.

1. Divide the following diphthongs into their component vowels. Use the basic vowel sounds: ee, eh, ah, oh, oo.

   Example: "a" in state = eh followed by ee

   A "a" in date = _____ followed by _____

   B "i" in write = _____ followed by _____

   C "o" in vote = _____ followed by _____

   D "ow" in cow = _____ followed by _____

   E "ow" in slow = _____ followed by _____

   F "y" in why = _____ followed by _____

   G "ou" in loud = _____ followed by _____

   H "ew" in view = _____ followed by _____

2. Find diphthong examples in your own music. List them below.

	Vowel		Word		1st Vowel		2nd Vowel
A	______	in	________	=	__________	followed by	__________
B	______	in	________	=	__________	followed by	__________
C	______	in	________	=	__________	followed by	__________
D	______	in	________	=	__________	followed by	__________

PHYSIOLOGY

NAME ____________________

DATE ____________________

The Breathing process: The physical aspect of breathing involves several different parts of the body.

During inhalation, the *diaphragm* muscle contracts, flattens and moves downward toward the feet. This motion pushes against the abdomen, pushing it outward. At the same time, the *intercostal muscles* (rib muscles) also contract, moving the ribs outward, expanding the rib cage. Since the lungs are attached to the diaphragm and the ribs, the lungs expand, and air rushes in. When you sing, your exhalation is controlled, the abdominal muscles contract and the ribs stay expanded to provide resistance and control to the exhalation.

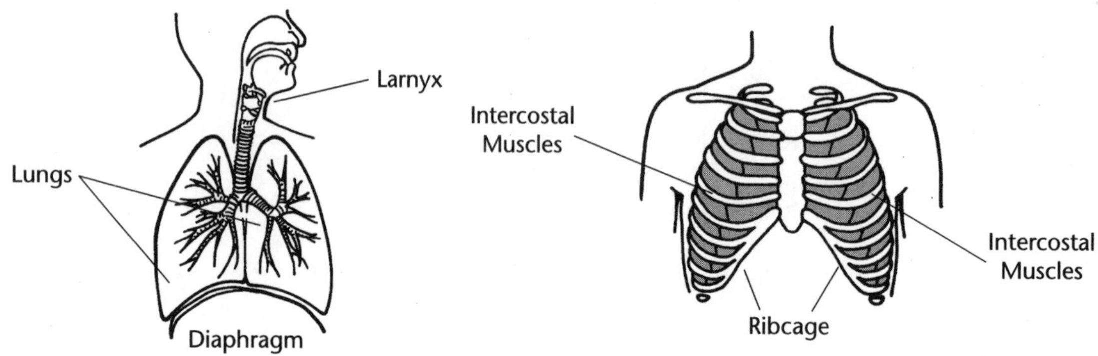

Vocalization: The source of vocal tone is the *larynx* (pronounced "LEH-rinks" and popularly called the "voice box" or "Adam's Apple"). The larynx is a part of the respiratory system and is not a muscle, but is made of *cartilage.* The larynx is located midway between the mouth, nose and throat above, and the lungs and trachea air passages below.

The Vocal Folds: The *vocal folds* (also called vocal cords) are a pair of muscles attached to the front and back of the larynx. They open and close somewhat like a valve – open for breathing, closed for singing (and speaking). Exhaled air passes between the gently closed vocal folds, causing them to vibrate. The number of vibrations per second produces pitch. The following illustration shows the vocal folds from above.

The Vocal Folds (seen from above)

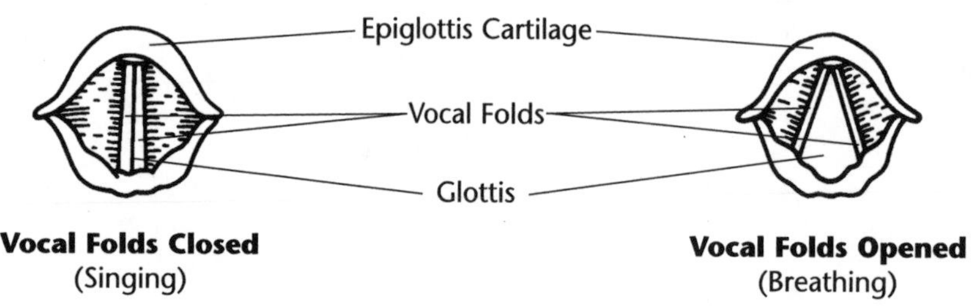

Vocal Folds Closed
(Singing)

Vocal Folds Opened
(Breathing)

PHYSIOLOGY QUIZ

NAME ______________________________

DATE ______________________________

BREATHING MECHANISM

Match the correct letter with the term.

1. _____ Diaphragm

2. _____ Lungs

3. _____ Intercostal Muscles

4. _____ Ribcage

5. _____ Larynx

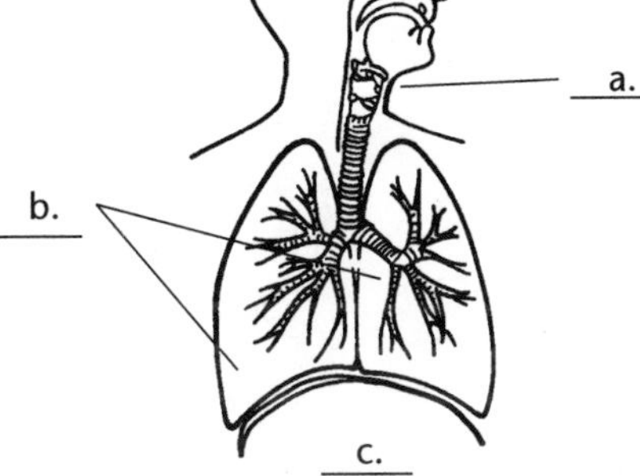

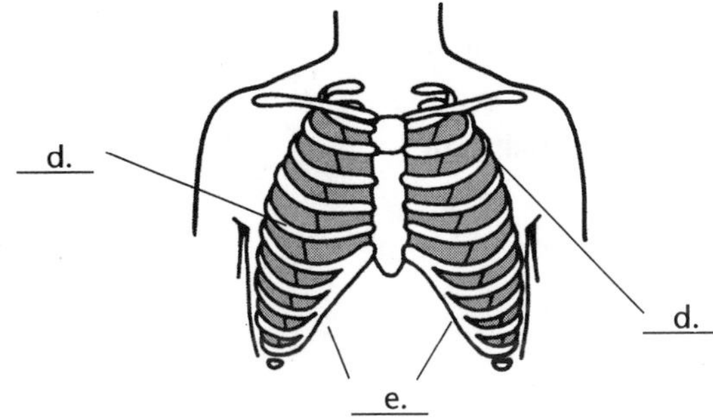

VOCAL MECHANISM

Match the correct letter with the term.

6. _____ Epiglottis Cartilage

7. _____ Vocal Folds

8. _____ Glottis

The Vocal Folds (seen from above)

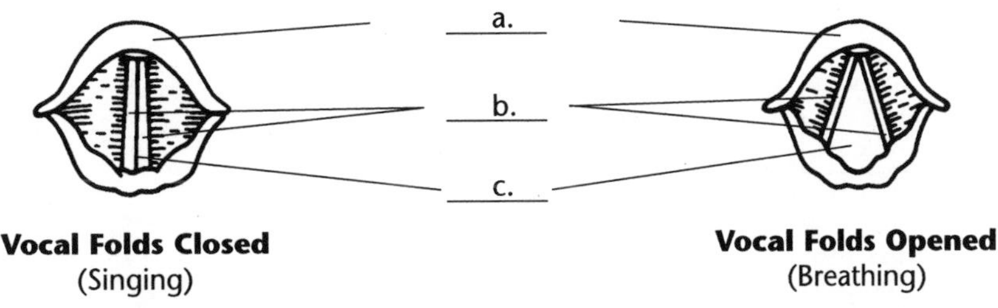

Vocal Folds Closed
(Singing)

Vocal Folds Opened
(Breathing)

BEAT, RHYTHM AND NOTATION

NAME ______________________________

DATE ______________________________

CHECK YOUR KNOWLEDGE

1. Define rhythm.
2. Define beat.
3. Write the following notes and rests.

A whole note	____	whole rest	____
B half note	____	half rest	____
C quarter note	____	quarter rest	____

THE SUM IS FOUR!

4. Add one quarter rest, half rest, or whole rest to each box to add up to 4 beats.

A [𝅗𝅥 ♩]

B [𝅗𝅥]

C [♩ ♩ ♩]

D [ ]

METER

NAME ____________________

DATE ____________________

CHECK YOUR KNOWLEDGE

1. __________ is a form of rhythmic organization.

2. In the meter signature, the top number indicates what?

3. In the meter signature, the bottom number indicates what?

WHAT DOES IT MEAN?

4. 4 = __________ beats per measure
   4 = __________ note receives the beat

5. 3 = __________ beats per measure
   4 = __________ note receives the beat

6. 2 = __________ beats per measure
   4 = __________ note receives the beat

ALL MIXED UP

Write the counts under each note. Then, read, tap or clap the exercise.

7. $\frac{4}{4}$

8. $\frac{3}{4}$

9. $\frac{2}{4}$

EIGHTH AND SIXTEENTH NOTES

NAME ____

DATE ____

CHECK YOUR KNOWLEDGE

1. Half the value of a quarter note is (a/an) ____________ note.

2. Half the value of an eighth note is (a/an) ____________ note.

3. If the quarter note receives the beat, the eighth notes are called a __________ of the beat.

4. If the quarter note receives the beat, the sixteenth notes are called a __________ of the beat.

5. Label the chart below with these words: division, subdivision, beat.

A ________

B ________

C ________

IT ALL COUNTS

Write the counts under each note. Then, read, tap, or clap the exercise.

6.

7.

8. 

KEY SIGNATURE – F MAJOR

NAME ________________________________

DATE ________________________________

CHECK YOUR KNOWLEDGE

1. The key of a piece is determined by ________ and ________.
2. In the key of F major, there is/are _________ flats (how many) in the key signature and the keynote is _________.
3. Name the pitches in F major.

A _ _ _ _ _

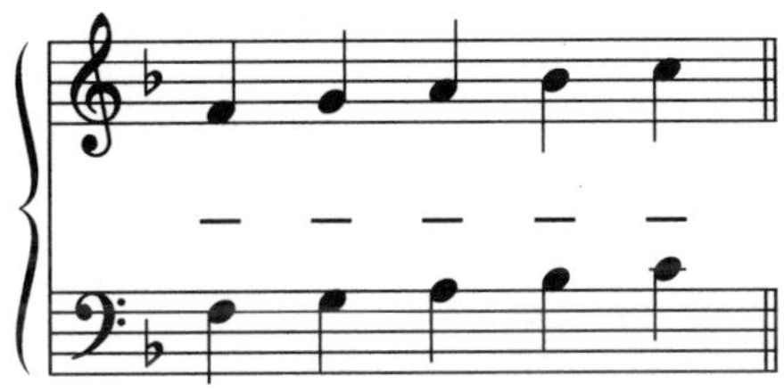

B _ _ _ _

CREATE YOUR OWN

On the blank staff below, write an original 4-bar melody in 4/4 meter in the key of F major. Write in a bass or treble clef sign, the key signature, and the time signature. Your melody may begin on *do, mi,* or *sol*, and should end on *do.*

TIES, SLURS, AND DOTTED QUARTER NOTES

NAME ______________________________

DATE ______________________________

CHECK YOUR KNOWLEDGE

1. T or F A *tie* connects two notes of the same pitch in order to extend the duration.

2. T or F A *slur* connects two notes of the same pitch in order to extend the duration.

3. Identify each of the following as a *tie* or a *slur*.

Ⓐ ______ Ⓑ ______ Ⓒ ______ Ⓓ ______

4. The dot increases the value of a note by __________.

5. Look at each set of notes and decide if they equal the same number of beats.

   Write "True" if they are equal and "False" if they are not equal.

   Ⓐ ______ ♩. ♪ = 𝅗𝅥

   Ⓑ ______ ♩. ♪ = ♩ ♩

   Ⓒ ______ ♩. ♪ = ♫

   Ⓓ ______ ♩. ♪ = ♫♫

6. Write the counts under each note. Then, read, clap or tap the exercise.

Ⓐ 

Ⓑ 

SYNCOPATION AND COMPOUND METER

NAME ______________________________

DATE ______________________________

CHECK YOUR KNOWLEDGE

1. Syncopation uses _________ and _________ to create rhythmic interest.

2. Write the counts under each note. Then, read, clap or tap the exercise.

A

B

COMPOUND METER

3. Write the counts under each note. Then, read, clap or tap the exercise.

A

B

FINDING THE MAJOR KEY

NAME ______________________________

DATE ______________________________

CHECK YOUR KNOWLEDGE

1. Describe the three rules used to determine the key of a piece based on the key signature.

   Rule 1 ______________________________

   ____

   ____

   ____

   Rule 2 ______________________________

   ____

   ____

   ____

   Rule 3 ______________________________

   ____

   ____

   ____

2. Based on the three rules, determine the key and keynote for the key signatures shown below.

   A Key of _____ major. Keynote is _____.

   B Key of _____ major. Keynote is _____.

   C Key of _____ major. Keynote is _____.

BASIC RHYTHMIC NOTATION

NAME ______________________________

DATE ______________________________

CHECK YOUR KNOWLEDGE

1. The organization of sound length (duration) is called ______________.

2. A steady recurring pulse is called the ______________________.

3. Identify the following notes.

   𝅝 = ______________ 𝅗𝅥 = ______________ ♩ = ______________

4. Practice writing the following notes.

   4 whole notes ____ ____ ____ ____

   4 half notes ____ ____ ____ ____

   4 quarter notes ____ ____ ____ ____

MUSICAL MATH

5. Compute the sum of the following "note problems" based on: ♩ = 1, 𝅗𝅥 = 2, 𝅝 = 4.

   Example: 𝅝 + 𝅗𝅥 + ♩ = 7

   4 + 2 + 1 = 7

   A ♩ + 𝅗𝅥 + ♩ + ♩ = ____

   B 𝅝 + ♩ + 𝅝 + ♩ = ____

   C ♩ + 𝅗𝅥 + 𝅝 + 𝅗𝅥 = ____

THE SUM IS FOUR!

6. Add one quarter, half, or whole note to each box to add up to 4 beats.

   A 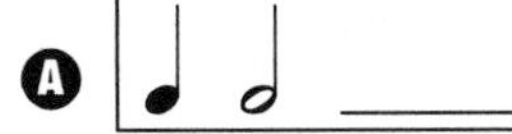 **B** 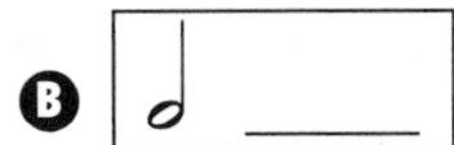 **C** ♩ ♩ ___ ♩

BASIC PITCH NOTATION – TREBLE CLEF

NAME ____

DATE ____

CHECK YOUR KNOWLEDGE

1. The five lines and four spaces on which music is written is called the ____________.

2. The symbol at the beginning of the staff that identifies a set of pitches is called a ____________.

3. Another name for the treble clef is the _______ clef.

4. Practice drawing the treble clef sign 5 times on the staff below.

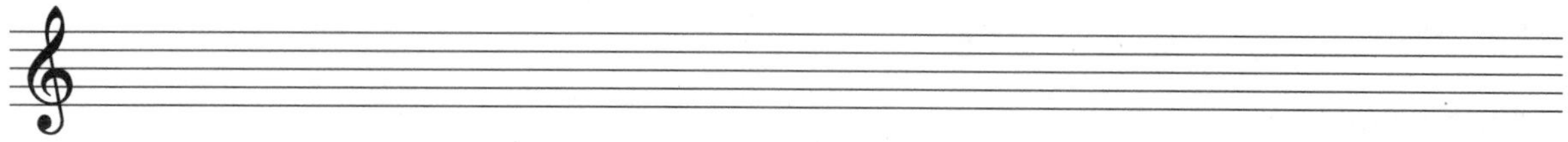

IDENTIFY PITCH NAMES

5. Identify the letter pitch names of the line and space notes in the treble clef.

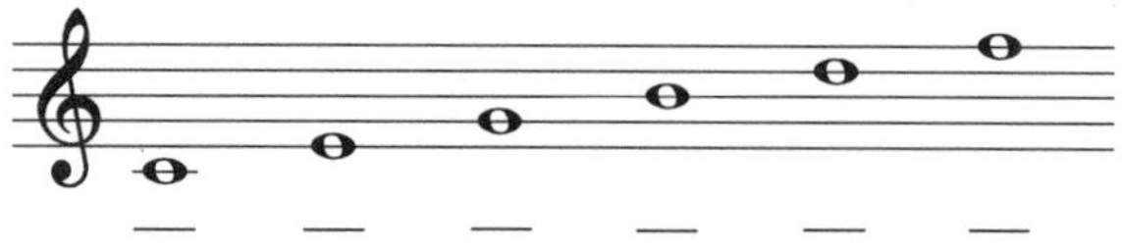

Line Notes

Space Notes

ON YOUR OWN!

6. Place a whole note on the correct line or space on the staff.

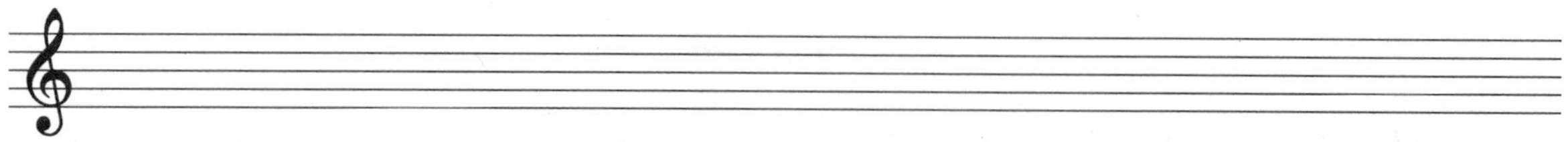

F(space) D(line) A(space) G(line) E(space) B(line) E(line) F(line)

BASIC PITCH NOTATION – BASS CLEF

NAME ____________________

DATE ____________________

CHECK YOUR KNOWLEDGE

1. There are _______ lines and _______ spaces in the musical staff.
2. The clef used for pitches below middle C is called the _______ clef.
3. Another name for the bass clef is the _______ clef.

PRACTICE TIME

4. Practice drawing the bass clef sign 5 times on the staff below.

IDENTIFY PITCH NAMES

5. Identify the letter pitch names of the line and space notes in the bass clef.

__ __ __ __ __

Line Notes

__ __ __ __ __

Space Notes

ON YOUR OWN!

6. Place a whole note on the correct line or space on the staff.

G(line) E(space) F(line) A(space) C(space) A(line) B(line) D(line)

MUSICAL SPELLING – TREBLE AND BASS CLEF

NAME ______________________________

DATE ______________________________

MUSICAL SPELLING – TREBLE CLEF

1. Name the notes in the treble clef. Each measure spells a word.

A

___ ___ ___ ___ ___ ___ ___

B

___ ___ ___

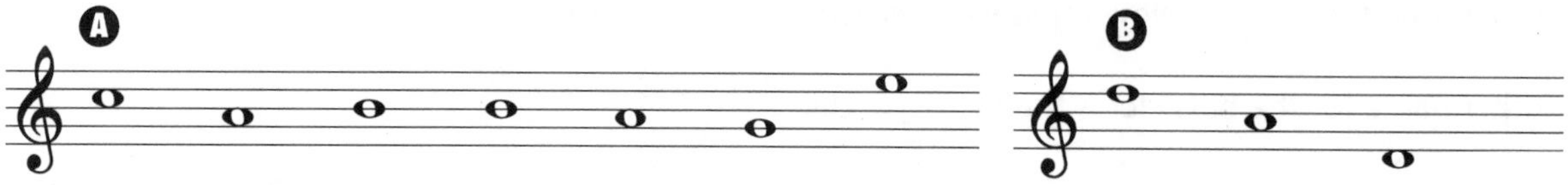

2. Place a whole note on the staff to spell each of the words. Write the treble clef on each staff.

A B E E F

B D E C A D E

C A G E

MUSICAL SPELLING – BASS CLEF

3. Name the notes in the bass clef. Each measure spells a word.

A

___ ___ ___ ___ ___ ___ ___

B

___ ___ ___

4. Place a whole note on the staff to spell each of the words. Write the bass clef on each staff.

A F A D E D

B F A C E

C B A D G E

METER AND TIME SIGNATURE

NAME ______________________________

DATE ______________________________

CHECK YOUR KNOWLEDGE

Matching: Write the letter of the definition that best describes the musical term in the blank next to that term.

_____ 1. bottom number
_____ 2. top number
_____ 3. meter
_____ 4. barline
_____ 5. double barline
_____ 6. time signature

A. Vertical line that divides the staff into smaller sections
B. Symbol at the beginning of the staff identifying the meter
C. Tells what note receives the beat
D. Symbol indicating the end of a section or a piece of music
E. A form of rhythmic organization
F. Tells how many beats per measure

WHAT DOES IT MEAN?

7. 4 = ________ beats per measure
   4 = ________ note receives the beat

8. 3 = ________ beats per measure
   4 = ________ note receives the beat

9. 2 = ________ beats per measure
   4 = ________ note receives the beat

COMPLETE THE MEASURE

Write one ♩, 𝅗𝅥 or 𝅝 to complete the measure. Check the time signature carefully.

10.

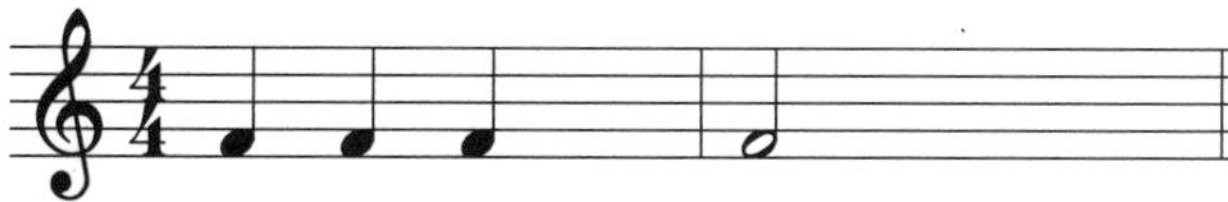

11.

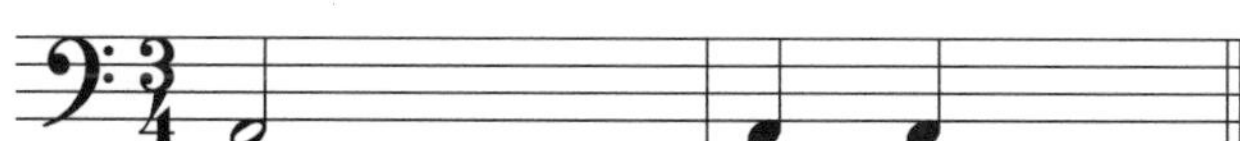

METER AND TIME SIGNATURE - PART 2

NAME ______________________________

DATE ______________________________

COMPLETE THE MEASURE

1. Write one ♩, 𝅗𝅥 or 𝅝 to complete the measure. Check the time signature carefully.

A 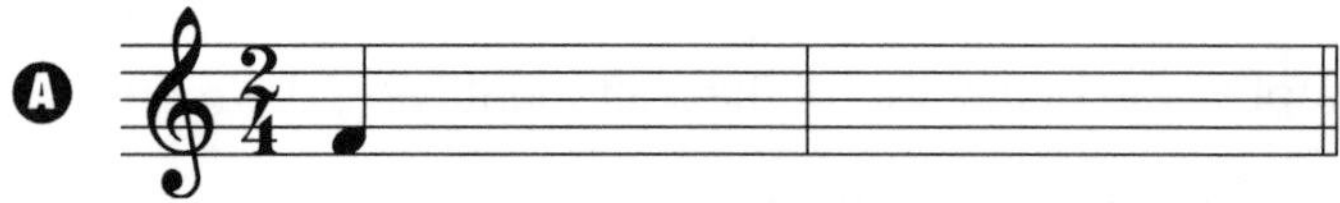

B 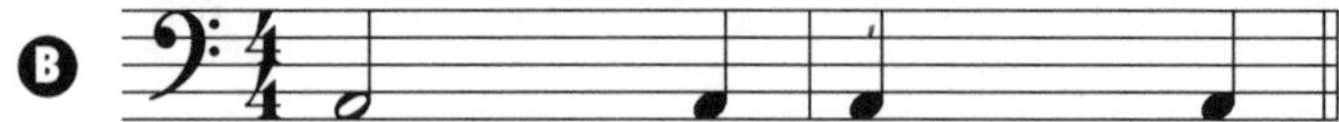

ADD THE BARLINES

2. Add the barlines to each line of rhythm so that each measure matches its time signature. Finish each line with the proper symbol.

A 

B 

C 

D 

KEY OF C MAJOR

NAME ____________________

DATE ____________________

Matching: Write the letter of the definition that best describes the musical term in the blank next to that term.

_____ 1. half step	A. Combination of two half steps side by side on the keyboard
_____ 2. scale	B. Highness or lowness of musical sound
_____ 3. key	C. Pitch which is the tonal center of a key (home tone)
_____ 4. whole step	D. Importance of one pitch over others in a scale
_____ 5. pitch	E. Specific arrangement of 5 whole and 2 half steps
_____ 6. major scale	F. Succession of higher and lower pitches (a "ladder")
_____ 7. grand staff	G. Smallest distance between 2 notes on a keyboard
_____ 8. keynote	H. Grouping of two staves – the treble and bass clefs together

THE C MAJOR SCALE

9. The key of C major has (how many) _____ sharps or flats in the key signature?

10. In the staff below, first label the pitch names of each note in the C major scale, then mark the whole and half steps. ⎵ = whole step ∨ = half step

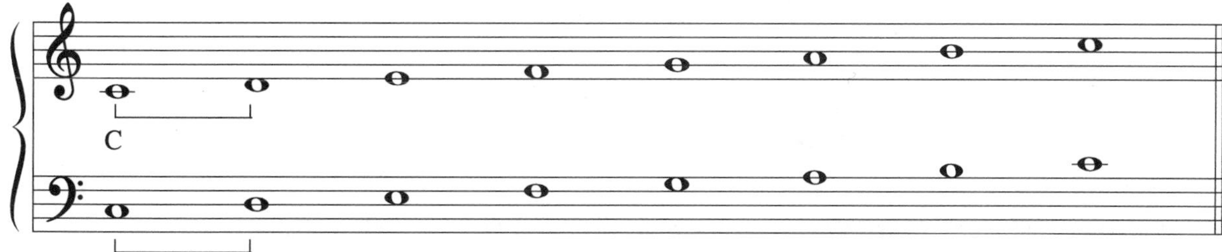

11. The half steps in the C major scale occur between the pitches ____ and ____ and the pitches _____ and _____.

KEY OF G MAJOR

NAME ____________________

DATE ____________________

CHECK YOUR KNOWLEDGE

1. A symbol which raises or lowers the pitch is an ____________________.

2. A ____________________ raises the pitch 1/2 step.

3. A ____________________ lowers the pitch 1/2 step.

4. The distance between two pitches is called an ____________________.

THE G MAJOR SCALE

5. In the staff below, label the pitch names of each note in the G major scale, place an accidental beside the correct note(s) in the scale, and mark the whole ⊔ and half ∨ steps.

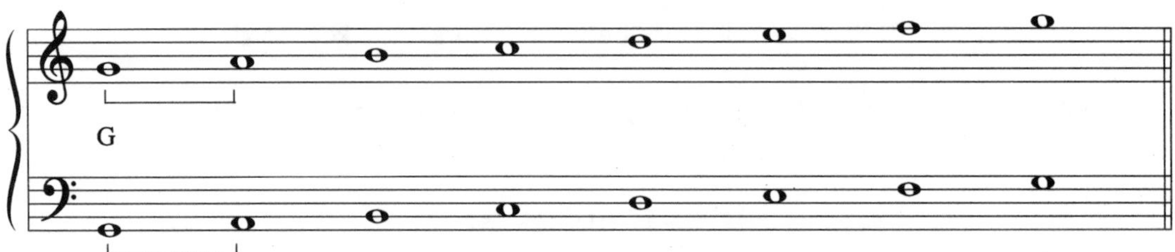

KEY SIGNATURE AND KEYNOTE OF G MAJOR

6. Write the key signature for the key of G major in the treble and bass clef, then place a whole note on the line or space which marks the keynote (tonic).

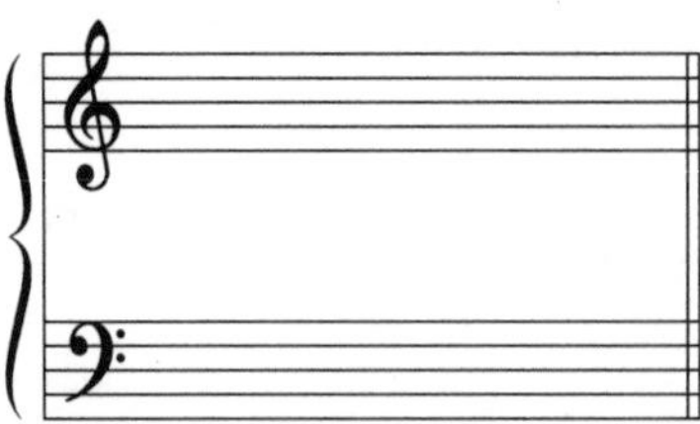

7. Whole Step or Half Step? Write "W" for each whole step, and "H" for each half step.

A) _____ G-A B) _____ A-B C) _____ B-C D) _____ C-D

E) _____ D-E F) _____ E-F♯ G) _____ F♯-G

THE "REST" IS UP TO YOU!

NAME ______________________________

DATE ______________________________

CHECK YOUR KNOWLEDGE

1. Silence in music is represented by the symbol of a ______________.

2. Identify the following rests. Based on 4/4 time signature, indicate how many beats of silence for each rest.

   A 𝄻 = ______________ = _____ beats of silence

   B 𝄼 = ______________ = _____ beats of silence

   C 𝄽 = ______________ = _____ beats of silence

THE REST

3. Write the rests on the staff.

   A four whole rests

   B four half rests

   C four quarter rests

FINISH THE MEASURE

4. Complete each measure using one rest per measure (𝄻 , 𝄼 , 𝄽)

   A 4/4 ♩ 𝅗𝅥 | ♩ ♩ | 𝅗𝅥 | ♩ ♩ ‖

   B 3/4 𝅗𝅥 | ♩ ♩ | 𝅗𝅥 | ♩ ‖

IT ALL ADDS UP

5. How many 𝄼 equal one 𝄻 ? _____

6. How many 𝄽 equal one 𝄼 ? _____

7. How many 𝄽 equal one 𝄻 ? _____

KEY OF F MAJOR

NAME ______________________________

DATE ______________________________

CHECK YOUR KNOWLEDGE

1. The key signature of F major has (how many) _______ flat(s).

2. The accidental is always placed to the LEFT or RIGHT (circle one) of a note.

3. Write the pitch names of the notes in the F major scale.

_____ _____ _____ _____ _____ _____ _____ _____

THE F MAJOR SCALE

4. In the staff below, label the pitch names of each note in the F major scale. Place an accidental beside the correct note(s) in the scale. Mark the whole ⊔ and half ∨ steps.

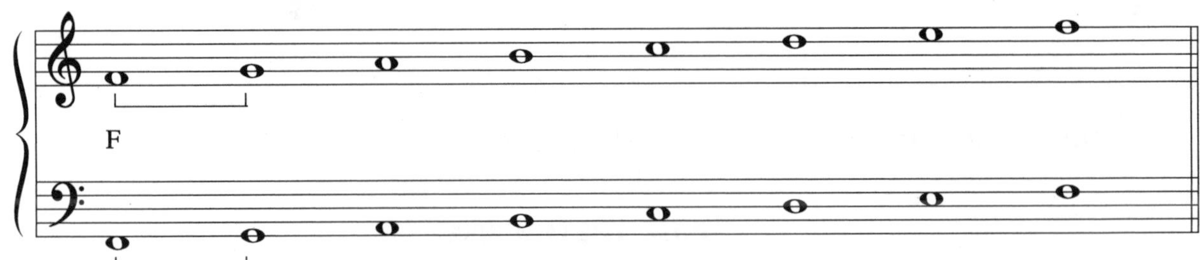

KEY SIGNATURE AND KEYNOTE OF F MAJOR

5. Write the key signature for the key of F major in the treble and bass clef, then place a whole note on the line or space which marks the keynote (tonic).

6. Bonus question. Arrange the dynamics in order from softest to loudest.

f mp p mf pp ff _____ _____ _____ _____ _____ _____

RHYTHM REVIEW - THE DOT

NAME ______________________________

DATE ______________________________

CHECK YOUR KNOWLEDGE

1. The dot after a note or rest adds ___________ the value of the note or rest to which it is attached.

2. The dot is placed to the RIGHT or LEFT (circle one) side of a note or rest.

3. Arrange the following notes in order from *greatest* value to *least* value:

FINISH THE MEASURES

4. Add a note , , , or a rest , , to complete each measure. Use only one note or rest per measure.

A 3/4

B 4/4

C 2/4

D 4/4

E 3/4

F 2/4

MUSICAL MATH

5. Find the sum of the notes based on quarter note = 1.

A + + + = ___________

B + + + = ___________

WHERE'S THE BARLINE?

6. Based on the time signature, divide these exercises into measures.

7. Create your own. On the back of this page create an original four-measure rhythm line. Use the notes, rests, and time signatures found on this worksheet. Be prepared to read, tap or clap your original exercise to the class.

RHYTHM PRACTICE - EIGHTH NOTES AND RESTS

NAME ______________________________

DATE ______________________________

CHECK YOUR KNOWLEDGE

1. In 4/4 time signature, an eighth note receives _______ beat(s) and an eighth rest receives _______ beat(s).

2. Eighth notes may be notated in two different ways. Write two of each.

3. Write four eighth rests.

4. Look at each set of notes and decide if they equal the same number of beats. Write "True" if they are equal and "False" if they are not equal.

A ___ =
B ___ =
C ___ =
D ___ =
E ___ =
F ___ =

KNOW THE TIME SIGNATURE

5. Fill in the box with the appropriate time signature for each exercise.

A
B
C

COMPLETE THE MEASURES

6. Complete each measure using notes and rests studied so far.

A 3/4
B 4/4

7. Write the counts under each note. Then read, tap, or clap the exercise.

4/4

BASIC RHYTHMIC NOTATION

NAME ____

DATE ____

CHECK YOUR KNOWLEDGE

1. The organization of sound length (duration) is called ______________.
2. A steady recurring pulse is called the ______________________.
3. Silence in music is represented by the symbol ____________.
4. Identify the following notes and rests. Give their value (how many beats) based on one quarter note or rest equals 1 beat.

   (A) 𝅝 = __________________ = _____ beats of sound

   (B) 𝅗𝅥 = __________________ = _____ beats of sound

   (C) ♩ = __________________ = _____ beats of sound

   (D) 𝄻 = __________________ = _____ beats of silence

   (E) 𝄼 = __________________ = _____ beats of silence

   (F) 𝄽 = __________________ = _____ beats of silence

IT ALL ADDS UP

5. How many 𝄼 equal one 𝄻 ? _____
6. How many ♩ equal one 𝅗𝅥 ? _____
7. How many 𝄽 equal one 𝄻 ? _____
8. How many 𝅗𝅥 equal one 𝅝 ? _____

MUSICAL MATH

9. Compute the sum of the following "note problems" based on: ♩ = 1, 𝅗𝅥 = 2, 𝅝 = 4.

Example: 𝅝 + 𝅗𝅥 + ♩ = 7

4 + 2 + 1 = 7

(A) ♩ + 𝅗𝅥 + ♩ + ♩ = _____

(B) 𝅗𝅥 + 𝅗𝅥 + 𝅗𝅥 = _____

BASIC RHYTHMIC NOTATION - PART 2

NAME

DATE

THE SUM IS FOUR!

1. Add one note to each box to add up to 4 beats.

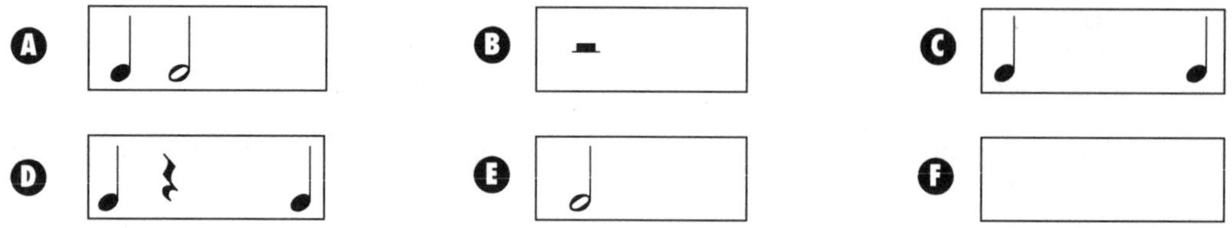

A B C

D E F

FINISH IT OFF!

2. Complete each measure using one rest per measure.

A 4/4

B 3/4

C 2/4

D 4/4

CREATE YOUR OWN!

3. Create your own original rhythmic line. Decide on the time signature. Then using the notes and rests you have studied so far, create a 4-measure exercise. Include barlines and a double barline at the end. Be prepared to read, tap or clap your original exercise to the class.

BASIC PITCH NOTATION

NAME ______________________________

DATE ______________________________

CHECK YOUR KNOWLEDGE

1. The graph on which music is written is called a ___________.
2. This graph is drawn with (how many) ______ lines and _____ spaces.
3. The grouping of the treble and bass clefs together is called the ______________________.
4. The clef that refers to pitches *above* middle C is called the ____________ clef.
5. The clef that refers to pitches *below* middle C is called the ____________ clef.
6. Another name for the treble clef is the _______ clef.
7. Another name for the bass clef is the _______ clef.
8. Identify the letter pitch names of the line and space notes in the treble clef.

Line Notes Space Notes

9. Identify the letter pitch names of the line and space notes in the bass clef.

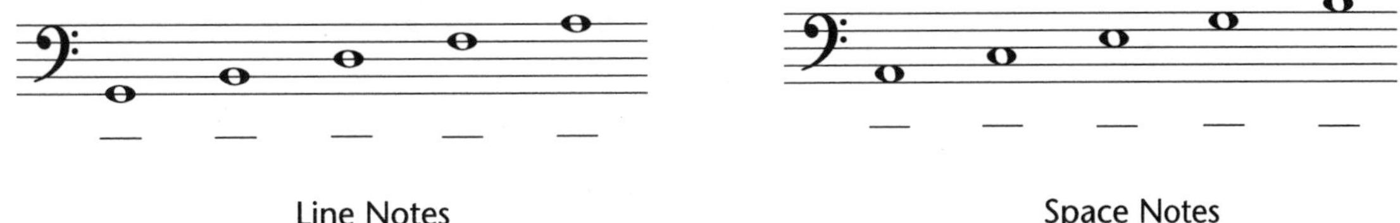

Line Notes Space Notes

MUSICAL SPELLING – TREBLE AND BASS CLEF

NAME ______________________________

DATE ______________________________

MUSICAL SPELLING – TREBLE CLEF

1. Name the notes in the treble clef. Each measure spells a word.

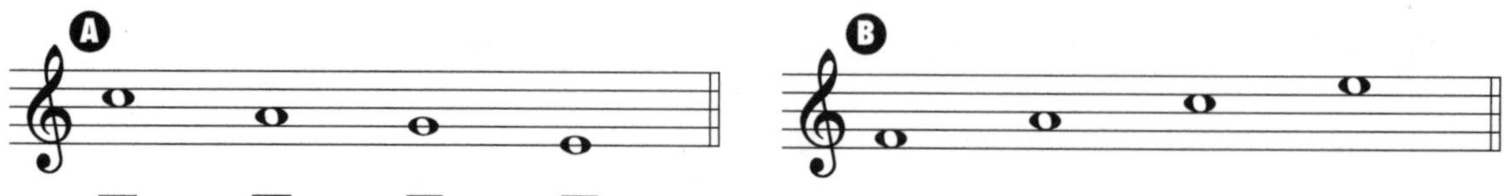

MUSICAL SPELLING – BASS CLEF

2. Name the notes in the bass clef. Each measure spells a word.

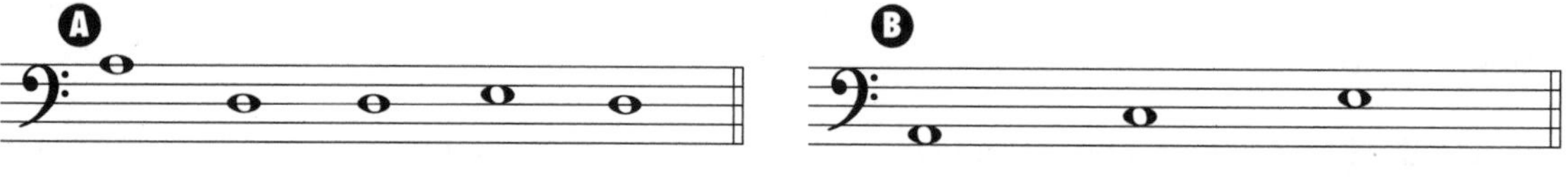

ALL MIXED UP!

3. Name the notes in the treble and bass clef. Each measure spells a word.

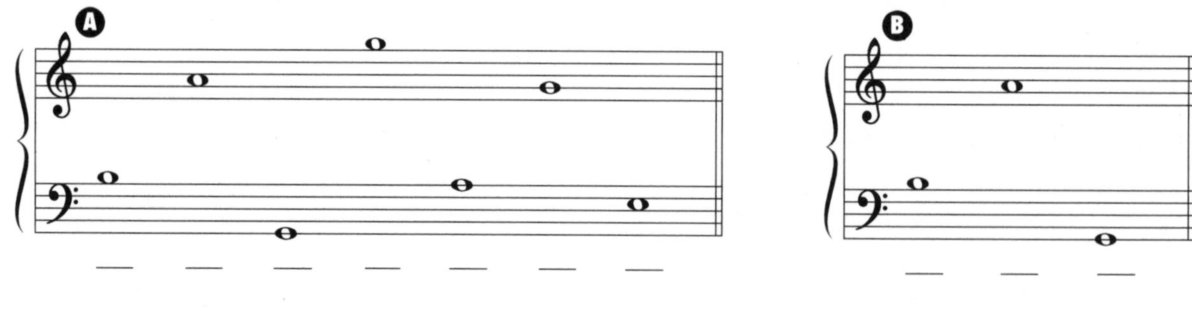

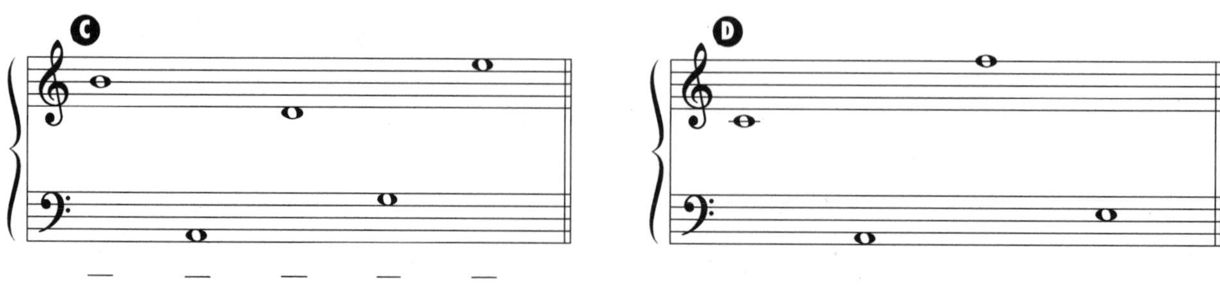

METER AND TIME SIGNATURE

NAME ____________________

DATE ____________________

CHECK YOUR KNOWLEDGE

Matching: Write the letter of the definition that best describes the musical term in the blank next to that term.

_____ 1. meter

_____ 2. top number

_____ 3. double barline

_____ 4. time signature

_____ 5. bottom number

_____ 6. barline

A. Vertical line that divides the staff into smaller sections

B. Symbol at the beginning of the staff identifying the meter

C. Tells what note receives the beat

D. Symbol indicating the end of a section or a piece of music

E. A form of rhythmic organization

F. Tells how many beats per measure

WHAT DOES IT MEAN?

7. 4 = ________ beats per measure
   4 = ________ note receives the beat

8. 3 = ________ beats per measure
   4 = ________ note receives the beat

9. 2 = ________ beats per measure
   4 = ________ note receives the beat

COMPLETE THE MEASURE

Write one ♩, 𝅗𝅥 or 𝅝 to complete the measure. Check the time signature carefully.

10. 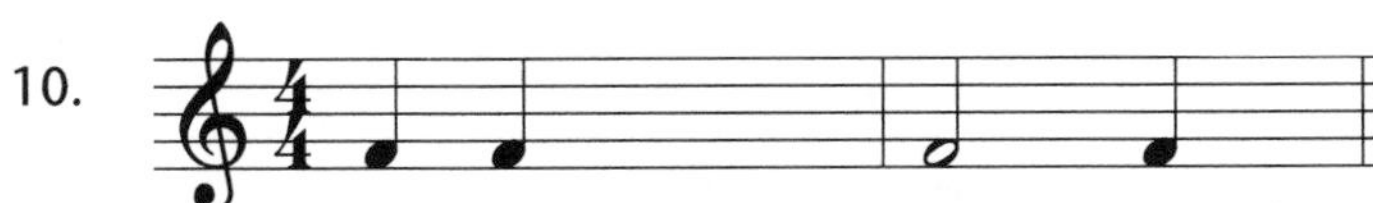

11. 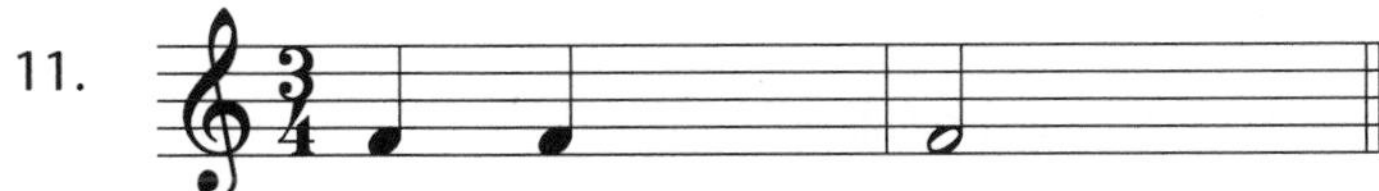

METER AND TIME SIGNATURE - PART 2

NAME ______________________________

DATE ______________________________

COMPLETE THE MEASURE

1. Write one ♩, 𝅗𝅥 or 𝅝 to complete each measure. Check the time signature carefully.

A 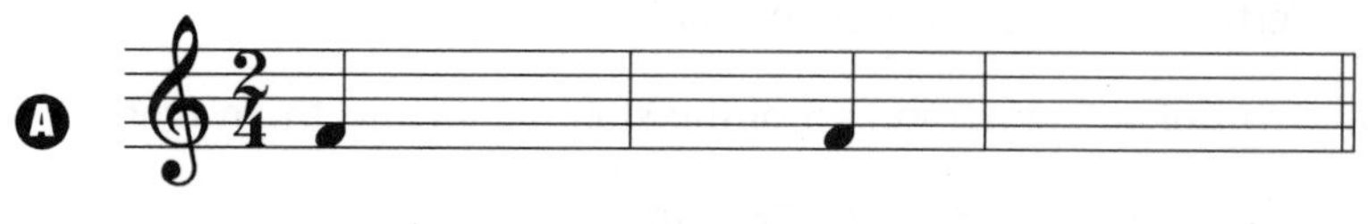

B 

ADD THE BARLINES

2. Add the barlines to each line of rhythm so that each measure matches its time signature. Finish each line with the proper symbol.

3. Practice reading the rhythm lines above by chanting, tapping or clapping the rhythms. For extra practice, conduct and count each line.

KEY OF C MAJOR

NAME ______________________________

DATE ______________________________

Matching: Write the letter of the definition that best describes the musical term in the blank next to that term.

_____ 1. octave — A. Combination of two half steps side by side on the keyboard

_____ 2. scale — B. Highness or lowness of musical sound

_____ 3. ledger line — C. Pitch which is the tonal center of a key (home tone)

_____ 4. whole step — D. Importance of one pitch over others in a scale

_____ 5. pitch — E. Specific arrangement of 5 whole and 2 half steps

_____ 6. major scale — F Succession of higher and lower pitches (a "ladder")

_____ 7. grand staff — G. Smallest distance between 2 notes on a keyboard

_____ 8. keynote — H. Grouping of two staves – the treble and bass clefs together

_____ 9. half step — I. Interval of eight scale tones

_____ 10. key — J. Short lines used to extend the range of the staff

THE C MAJOR SCALE

11. Label the pitch names of each note in the C major scale. Mark the whole and half steps in the scale.

⊔ = whole step   ∨ = half step

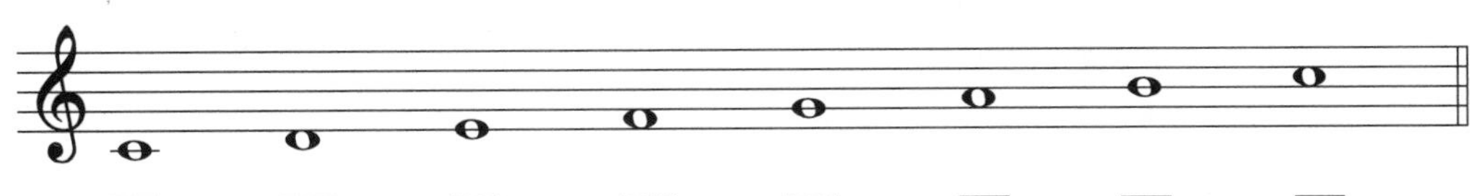

12. Whole Step or Half Step? Write "W" for each whole step, and "H" for each half step as found in the C major scale.

A _____ C-D   **B** _____ D-E   **C** _____ E-F   **D** _____ F-G

E _____ G-A   **F** _____ A-B   **G** _____ B-C

KEY OF G MAJOR

NAME ____________________

DATE ____________________

CHECK YOUR KNOWLEDGE

1. A symbol not in the key signature which raises or lowers the pitch is called what?

2. A ____________________ raises the pitch 1/2 step.

3. A ____________________ lowers the pitch 1/2 step.

THE G MAJOR SCALE

4. Label the pitch names of each note in the G major scale. Place an accidental beside the correct note(s) in the scale for the key of G major. Mark the whole ⊔ and half ∨ steps in the scale.

THE KEY SIGNATURE AND KEYNOTE OF G MAJOR

5. Write the key signature for the key of G major in the treble and bass clef, then place a whole note on the line or space which marks the keynote (tonic).

6. Whole Step or Half Step? Write "W" for each whole step, and "H" for each half step.

   A _____ G-A **B** _____ A-B **C** _____ B-C **D** _____ C-D

   E _____ D-E **F** _____ E-F♯ **G** _____ F♯-G

INTERVALS

NAME ______________________________

DATE ______________________________

CHECK YOUR KNOWLEDGE

1. The measurement of distance between two pitches is called an ______________.

2. When intervals are played in succession they are called ____________ intervals.

3. Intervals played simultaneously are called ___________ intervals.

MELODIC INTERVALS

4. Identify these melodic intervals.

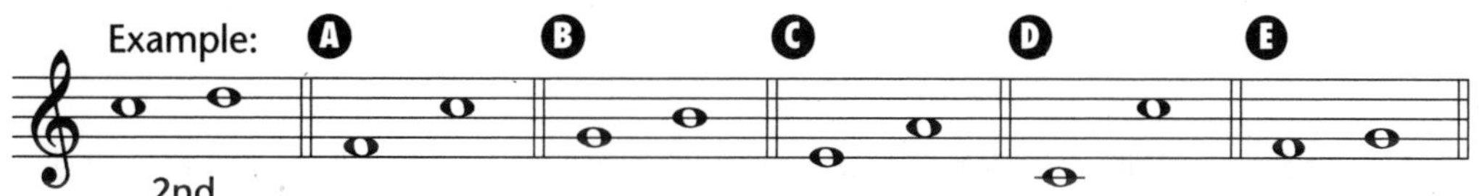

5. Bass Clef Practice

HARMONIC INTERVALS

6. Write a whole note on the staff above the given note to create the harmonic interval indicated in the treble clef.

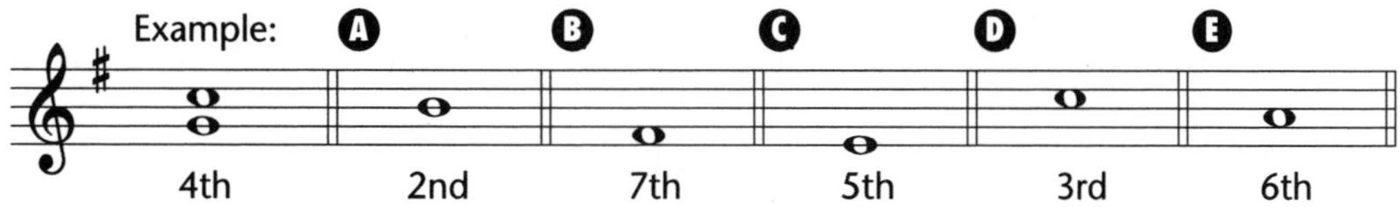

7. Bass Clef Practice

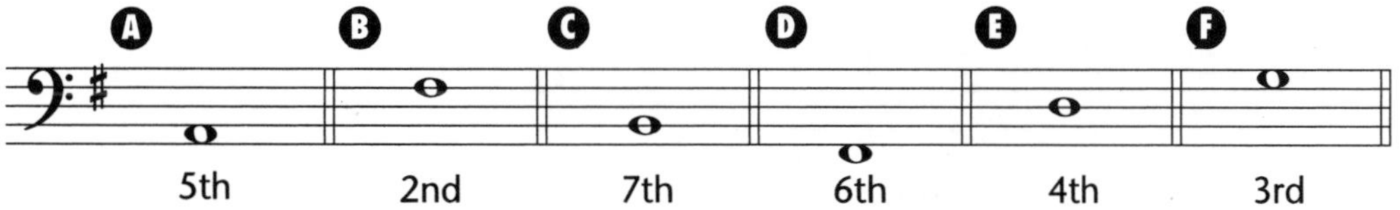

KEY OF F MAJOR

NAME ____________________

DATE ____________________

THE F MAJOR SCALE

1. Label the pitch names of each note in the F major scale. Place an accidental beside the correct note(s) in the scale. Mark the whole ⊔ and half ∨ steps in the scale.

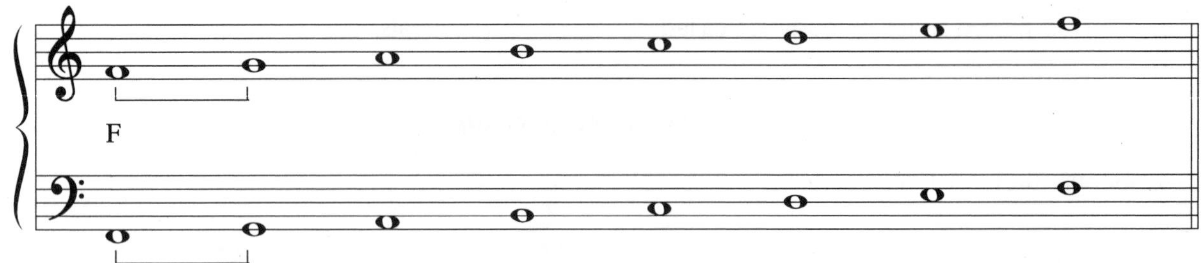

2. Whole Step or Half Step? Write "W" for each whole step, and "H" for each half step as found in the F major scale.

3. How many flats are in the key signature for F major? __________

4. When writing the key signature for F major in the treble clef, the flat is placed on which line of the staff? __________

5. When writing the key signature for F major in the bass clef, the flat is placed on which line of the staff? __________

6. Identify the chords below as tonic or dominant in the key of F major. Give the symbol.

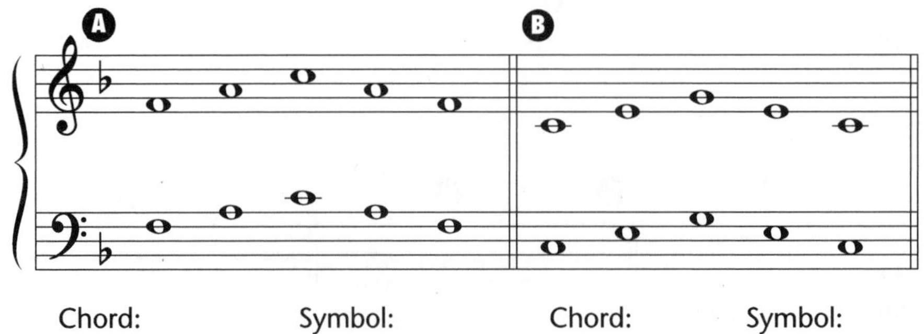

Chord: Symbol: Chord: Symbol:

KEY OF D MAJOR

NAME ______________________________

DATE ______________________________

THE D MAJOR SCALE

1. Label the pitch names of each note in the D major scale. Place an accidental beside the correct note(s) in the scale. Mark the whole ⊔ and half ∨ steps in the scale.

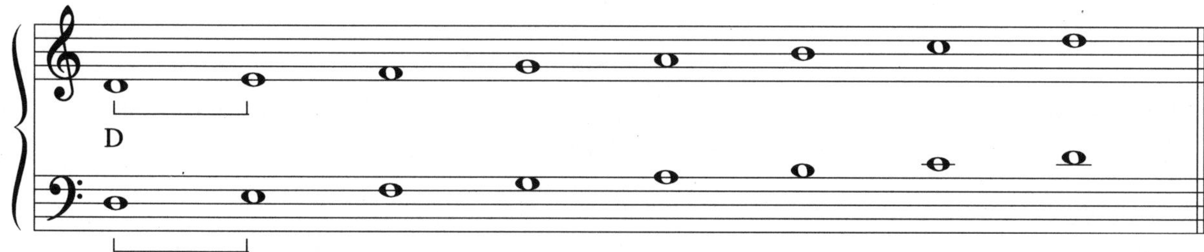

THE KEY SIGNATURE AND KEYNOTE OF D MAJOR

2. Write the key signature for the key of D major in the treble and bass clef, then place a whole note on the line or space that marks the keynote (tonic).

3. Identify the chords below as tonic, dominant or subdominant in the key of D major. Give the symbol.

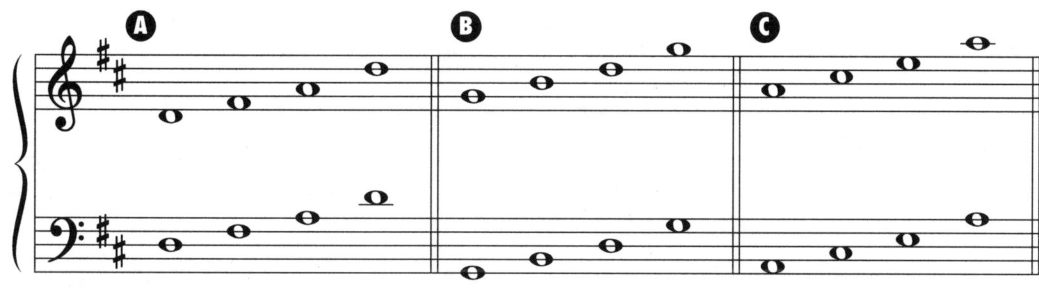

Chord: Symbol: Chord: Symbol: Chord: Symbol:

KEY OF B♭ MAJOR

NAME ______________________________

DATE ______________________________

CHECK YOUR KNOWLEDGE

1. The key of B♭ Major has (how many) ________ flats in the key signature.
2. The pitch names of those flats are _______ and _______.

THE B♭ MAJOR SCALE

3. Label the pitch names of each note in the B♭ major scale. Place an accidental beside the correct note(s) in the scale. Mark the whole ⊔ and half ∨ steps in the scale.

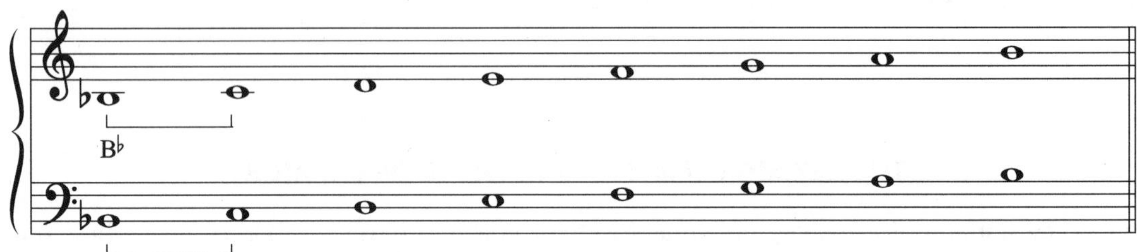

THE KEY SIGNATURE AND KEYNOTE OF B♭ MAJOR

4. Write the key signature for the key of B♭ major in the treble and bass clef. Place a whole note on the line or space that marks the keynote (tonic).

5. Identify the chords below as tonic, dominant or subdominant. Give the symbol.

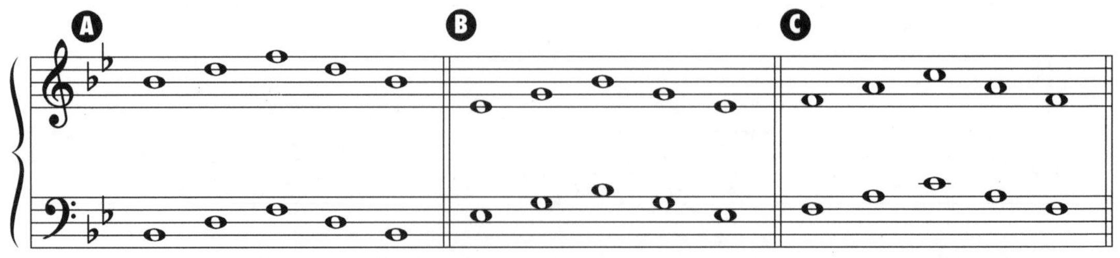

Chord: Symbol: Chord: Symbol: Chord: Symbol:

RHYTHM PRACTICE

NAME ______________________________

DATE ______________________________

CHECK YOUR KNOWLEDGE

1. In 4/4 time signature, an eighth note receives _________ beat(s).

2. Eighth notes may be notated in two different ways. Give an example of each.

3. Sixteenth notes may be notated in two different ways. Give an example of each.

4. Write an eighth rest ______________. A sixteenth rest ______________.

5. Look at each set of notes and decide if they are equal in value. Write "True" if they are equal and write "False" if they are not equal.

A ____ B ____ C ____

D ____ E ____ F ____

COMPLETE THE MEASURES

6. Complete each measure using notes and rests studied so far.

COUNT ON ME!

7. Write the counts under each note. Then read, tap, or clap the exercise.

RELATIVE MINOR SCALE

NAME ______________________________

DATE ______________________________

CHECK YOUR KNOWLEDGE

1. The central tone around which tonal music is organized is known as the keynote or the ____________________.

2. The smallest distance between two notes is a _________ step.

3. A combination of two half steps is a ____________ step.

4. Relative major and minor keys share the same _______ signature.

5. The relative minor scale is based on what degree of the major scale?

THE A MINOR SCALE

6. Label the pitch names of each note in the A minor scale, then mark the whole ⊔ and half ∨ steps in the scale.

A

7. The half steps in the A minor scale occur between which pitches?

A _______ and ________ **B** ________ and _________

8. Discuss how the arrangement of whole steps and half steps differ between the major scale and the relative minor scale.

RELATIVE MINOR SCALES - PART 2

NAME ______________________________

DATE ______________________________

NAME THAT KEY

1. In each example below, identify the major key by looking at the key signature. Then identify the relative minor key. Place a whole note on the line or space which marks the keynote (tonic) of each key. Remember: The relative minor scale is based on the 6th scale degree of its relative major scale.

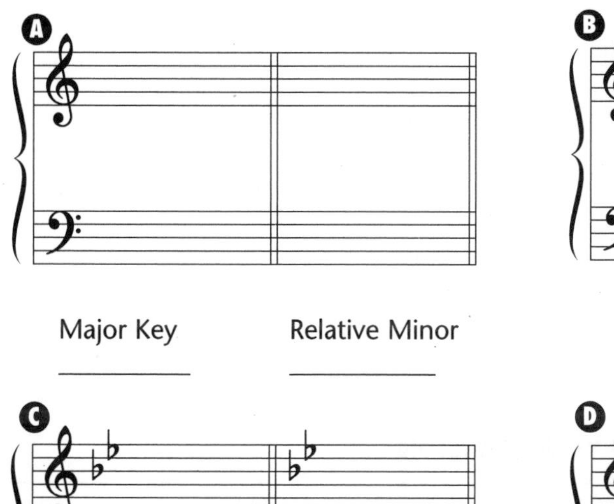

A — Major Key ________ Relative Minor ________

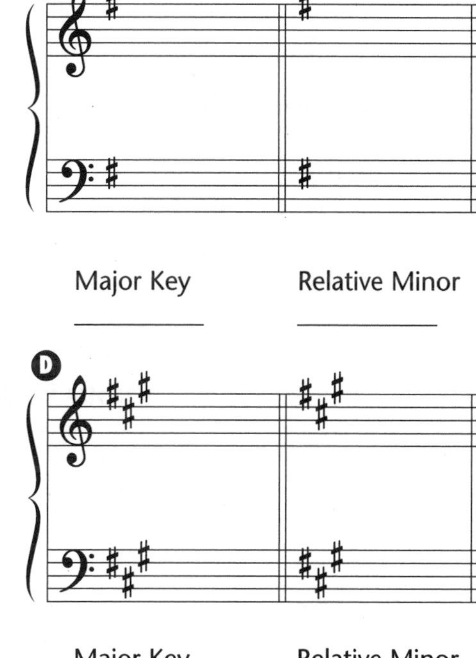

B — Major Key ________ Relative Minor ________

C — Major Key ________ Relative Minor ________

D — Major Key ________ Relative Minor ________

NATURAL MINOR SCALE

2. Identify the relative minor key. Using whole notes, write an ascending natural minor scale in that key. Mark the whole ⊔ and half ∨ steps in the scale.

Minor key:

RHYTHMIC NOTATION

NAME ______________________________

DATE ______________________________

CHECK YOUR KNOWLEDGE

1. The organization of rhythm in music is called the _________.

2. Another name for meter is ____________ ____________________.

3. Fill in the blanks.

A 3 = _______ beats per measure
8 = _______ note receives the beat

B 2 = _______ beats per measure
4 = _______ note receives the beat

C 3 = _______ beats per measure
2 = _______ note receives the beat

KNOW YOUR DIVISION

Beat	Division	Subdivision
3/2		
3/4		
2/8		

ADD THE BARLINES

4. Based on the time signature given, add the barlines to each rhythm exercise.

A 4/4

B 3/4

INTERVALS

NAME ____________________

DATE ____________________

CHECK YOUR KNOWLEDGE

1. The measurement of the distance between two notes is called an __________.

2. Pitches played in succession are called __________ intervals.

3. Pitches played simultaneously are called __________ intervals.

4. Identify each interval by its abbreviation.

   A "M" = __________ interval

   B "m" = __________ interval

   C "P" = __________ interval

   D "dim" = __________ interval

5. Label the intervals above the tonic in the C major scale. Use the abbreviation for the interval (P4, M2, m2, P5, dim3).

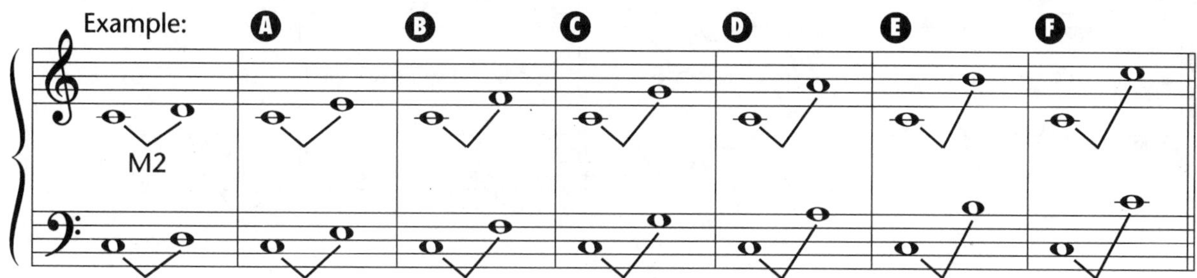

6. Label the intervals above the tonic in the C minor scale. Use the abbreviation for the interval (P4, M2, m2, P5, dim3).

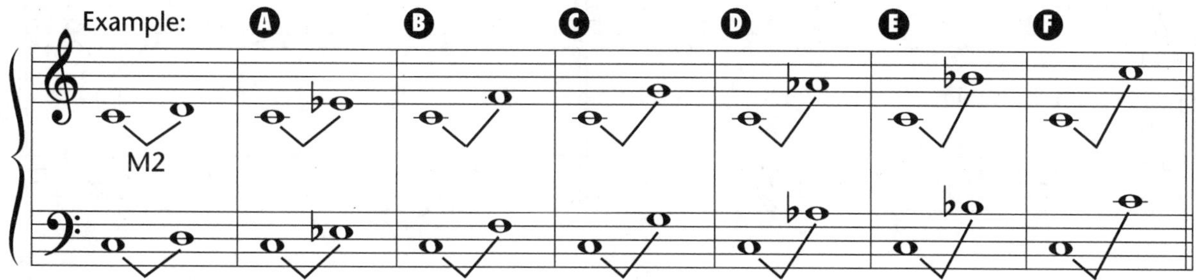

INTERVALS – PART 2

NAME ____________________

DATE ____________________

CHECK YOUR KNOWLEDGE

1. Identify the following intervals.

   A ______________ is a major interval that is decreased by 1/2 step.

   B ______________ is a major interval that is increased by 1/2 step.

   C ______________ is a perfect interval that is decreased by 1/2 step.

   D ______________ is a perfect interval that is increased by 1/2 step.

REWRITE THE INTERVAL

2. The first interval in each example below is a major interval. Add an accidental to the second interval so that it becomes a minor interval.

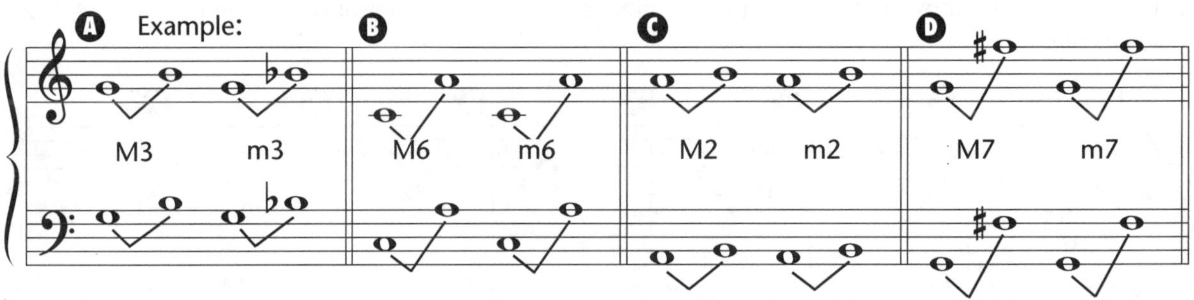

3. The first interval in each example below is a perfect interval. Add an accidental to the second interval so that it becomes either diminished or augmented as requested.

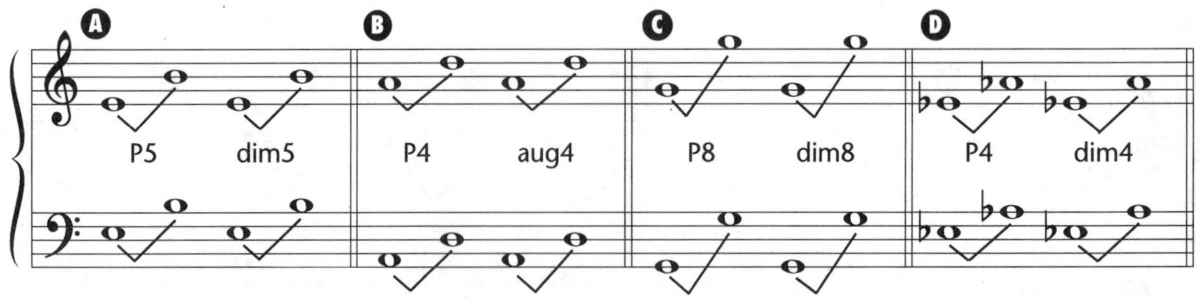

CATEGORIES OF HARMONY

NAME ____________________

DATE ____________________

CHECK YOUR KNOWLEDGE

1. Based on the description, give the chord name, type and symbol.

Description	Chord Name	Chord Type	Chord Symbol
Home, at ease, at rest	tonic	major	I
Energy, momentum toward tonic			
Strongest and smallest progression toward the tonic			
Chord midway between tonic and dominant			
Chord immediately above tonic			
Digression, diversion away from tonic			
Chord below tonic, midway between it and the dominant			

IDENTIFY THE CHORDS

2. Based on the key signature, identify the chords. Place the chord symbol below each chord.

Chord: ___ ___ ___ ___ ___ ___ ___ ___

CATEGORIES OF HARMONY - PART 2

NAME ____________________

DATE ____________________

BUILDING TRIADS

1. Build the triads indicated in both the treble and bass clefs using whole notes.

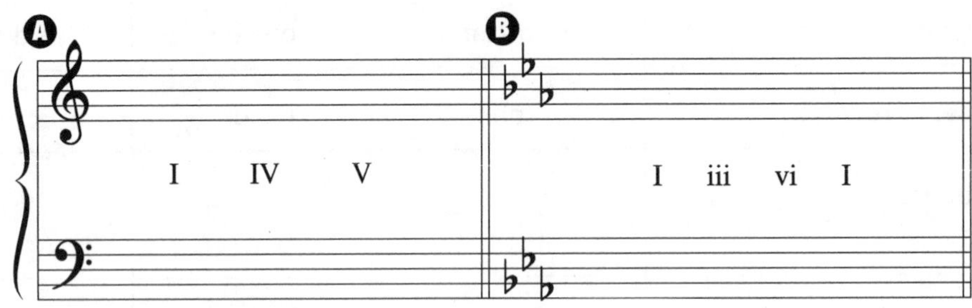

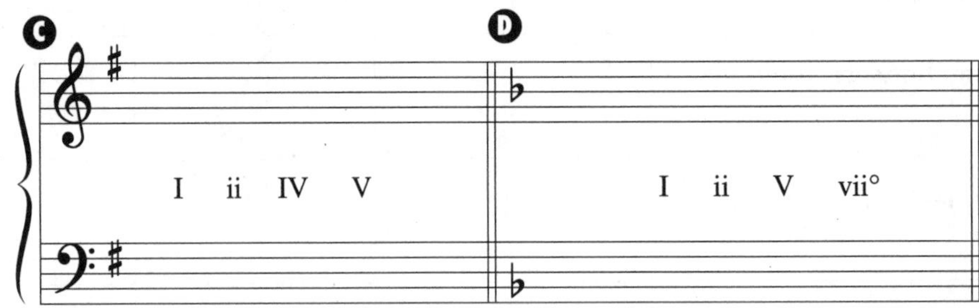

ANALYZE THE CHORDS

2. Analyze the chords in each measure and determine the chord symbol for each.

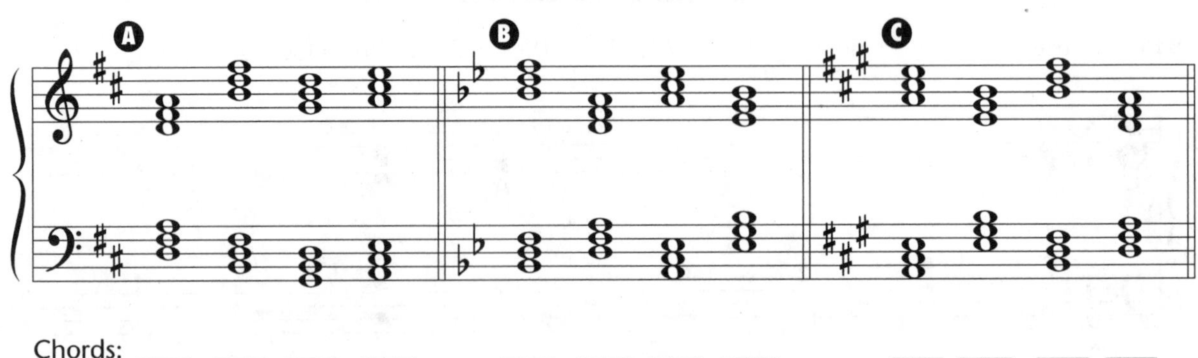

Chords: ___ ___ ___ ___ ___ ___ ___ ___ ___ ___ ___ ___

COMPOUND METER

NAME ______________________________

DATE ______________________________

CHECK YOUR KNOWLEDGE

1. Another name for meter is ______________ ______________.

2. When the top number of a time signature is any number divisible by three, except for three itself, it is referred to as what kind of meter?

3. Which meter uses a multiple of three and measures the division of the beat?

4. Look at each set of notes and decide if they are equal in value. Write "True" if they are equal and write "False" if they are not equal.

A ____ 𝅗𝅥. = ♩♩♩ B ____ ♩♪♩♪ = ♩. ♩. C ____ ♩♪♫ = ♩. ♩ ♪

D ____ ♩. = ♫♫ E ____ ♩. 𝄽. = 𝄾♫𝄾♫ F ____ ♫♩♩. = ♫𝄾♩ ♩ ♪

IDENTIFY METER

5. Fill in the blanks. Based on what you have learned, identify each meter as simple or compound. Circle your answer.

A 3 = ____ beats per measure simple or compound
4 = ____ note receives the beat

B 12 = ____ beats per measure simple or compound
8 = ____ note receives the beat

C 8 = ____ beats per measure simple or compound
4 = ____ note receives the beat

D 9 = ____ beats per measure simple or compound
4 = ____ note receives the beat

E 6 = ____ beats per measure simple or compound
4 = ____ note receives the beat

F 6 = ____ beats per measure simple or compound
8 = ____ note receives the beat

COMPOUND METER – PART 2

NAME ______________________________

DATE ______________________________

COMPLETE THE MEASURES

1. Add notes and rests to the measures below so that each is complete based on its time signature.

ADD THE BARLINES

2. Add the barlines so that each measure matches its time signature.

CREATE YOUR OWN

3. Write an original 4-measure rhythm line using compound meter. Be prepared to perform your composition for the class.

ACCIDENTALS

NAME ______________________________

DATE ______________________________

CHECK YOUR KNOWLEDGE

1. A ____________________ returns a specific pitch to its original unaltered pitch.

2. Half steps which are created by notes altered by an accidental yet retain their same pitch names are called what?

3. What are half steps using different pitch names called?

IDENTIFY THE HALF STEPS

4. In the exercises below write the letter "C" for the *chromatic* half steps and the letter "D" for the *diatonic* half steps.

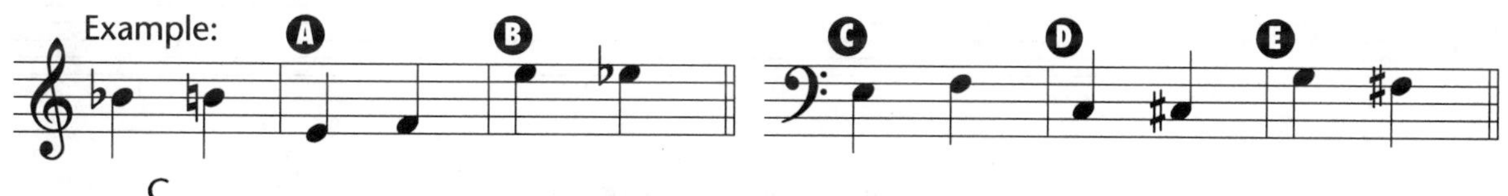

WRITE THE HALF STEPS

5. In the staff below fill in the missing notes to create an ascending *chromatic* half step or *diatonic* half step, depending on what is asked.

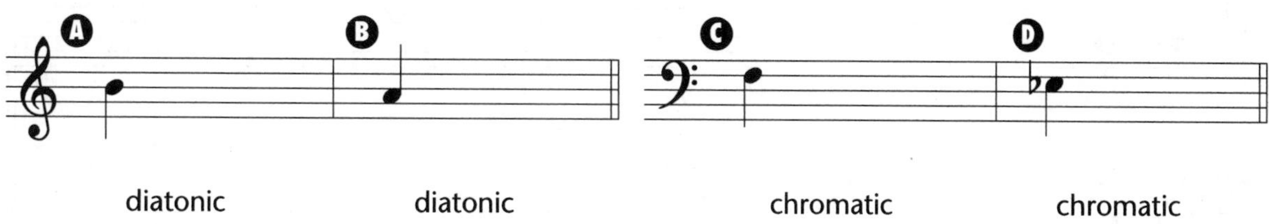

DIATONIC AND CHROMATIC SCALES

NAME ______________________________

DATE ______________________________

CHECK YOUR KNOWLEDGE

THE DIATONIC SCALE

1. The diatonic scale uses __________ half steps which have ______________ pitch names.

2. Give an example of a diatonic scale. ___________________________

3. Using whole notes, write an ascending diatonic scale for the key and tonic given. Mark the whole ⊔ and half ∨ steps in the scale.

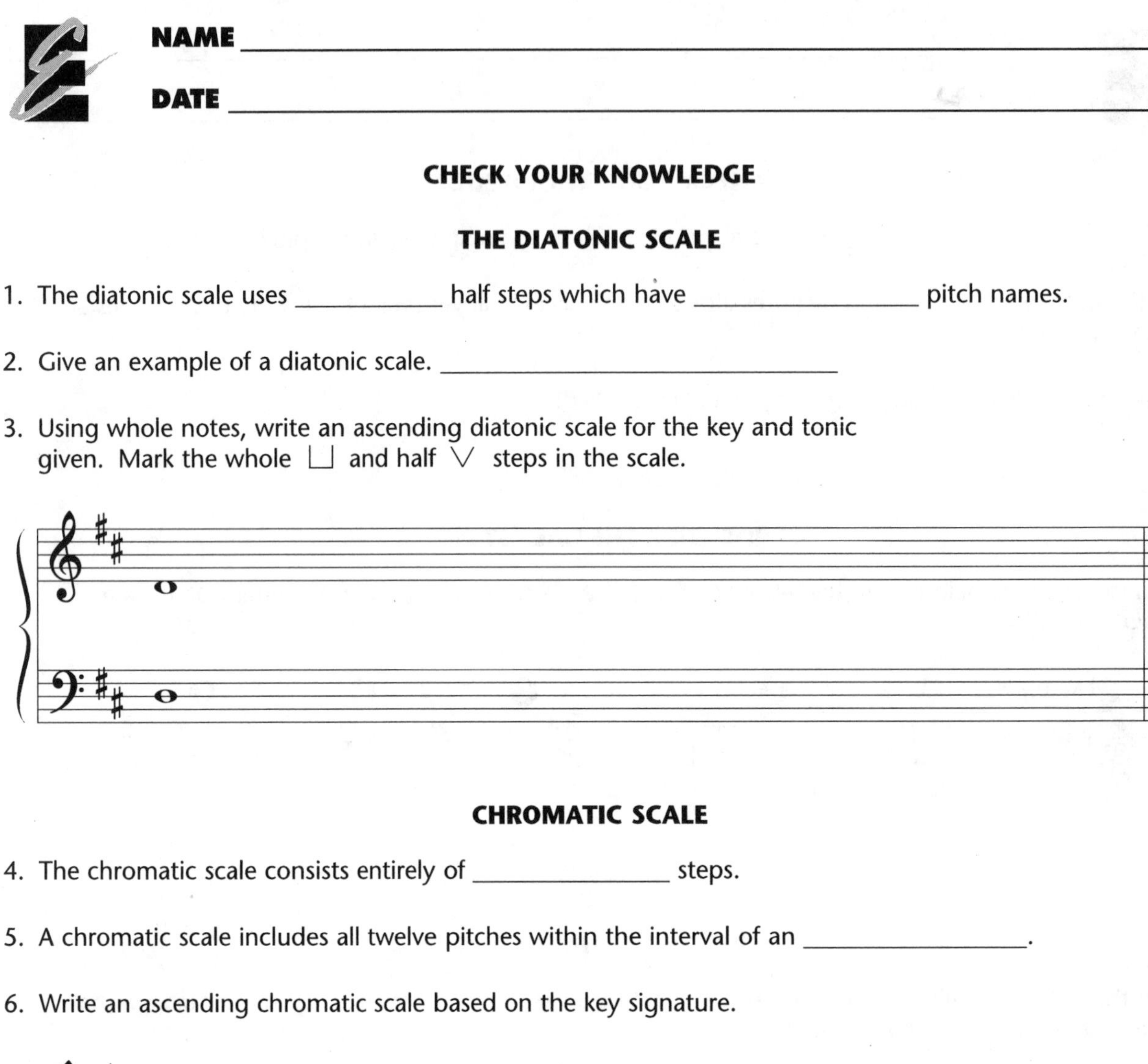

CHROMATIC SCALE

4. The chromatic scale consists entirely of _____________ steps.

5. A chromatic scale includes all twelve pitches within the interval of an _______________.

6. Write an ascending chromatic scale based on the key signature.

HARMONIC AND MELODIC MINOR SCALES

NAME ____________________

DATE ____________________

CHECK YOUR KNOWLEDGE

1. Name three categories of the minor scale.

   A ____________ **B** ____________ **C** ____________

2. When the 7th degree of a natural minor scale is raised a half step, what type of minor scale is created?

3. In an ascending melodic minor scale, both the _______ and _______ degrees are raised a half step, and returned to their natural minor positions when the scale descends.

THE HARMONIC MINOR SCALE

4. Add an accidental(s) to the natural minor scale to create a harmonic minor scale. Mark the whole ⊔ and half ∨ steps in the scale.

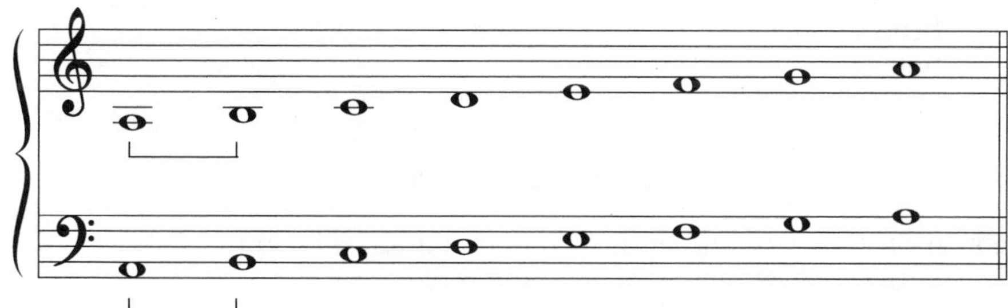

THE MELODIC MINOR SCALE

5. Add an accidental(s) to the ascending and descending natural minor scale to create a melodic minor scale. Mark the whole ⊔ and half ∨ steps in the scale.

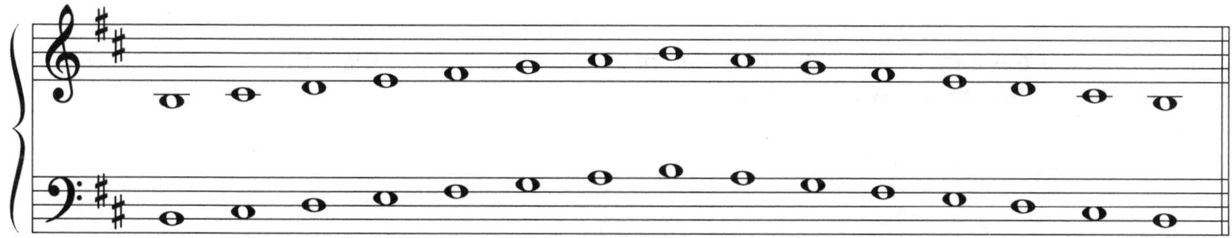

ASYMMETRIC METER

NAME ______________________________

DATE ______________________________

CHECK YOUR KNOWLEDGE

1. The organization of rhythm in music is called ________________.

2. Another name for meter is ____________ ________________.

3. What kind of meter uses strong beats which create combinations of groups of twos and threes?

4. Fill in the blanks, then identify each meter as simple, compound, or asymmetric.

A 2 = _______ beats per measure meter:
4 = _______ note receives the beat

B 5 = _______ beats per measure meter:
4 = _______ note receives the beat

C 6 = _______ beats per measure meter:
8 = _______ note receives the beat

D 7 = _______ beats per measure meter:
8 = _______ note receives the beat

ADD THE BARLINES

5. Based on the meter in each example, finish the line of rhythm by adding the barlines. Show the combinations of groups of twos and threes.

A 5/8 (3 2)

B 7/8 (2 2 3)

6. On the back of this page, create your own line of asymmetric rhythm. Mark the combinations of groups of twos and threes.

TREBLE/BASS SIGHT READING TESTS

NAME ______________________________

DATE ______________________________

1 p. 15

2 p. 35

3 p. 55

4 p. 88

5 p. 15

6 p. 35

7 p. 55

8 p. 88

TREBLE SIGHT READING TESTS

NAME ______________________________

DATE ______________________________

(1) p. 14

(2) p. 27

(3) p. 46

(4) p. 66

(5) p. 84

(6) p. 91

(7) p. 100

(8) p. 123

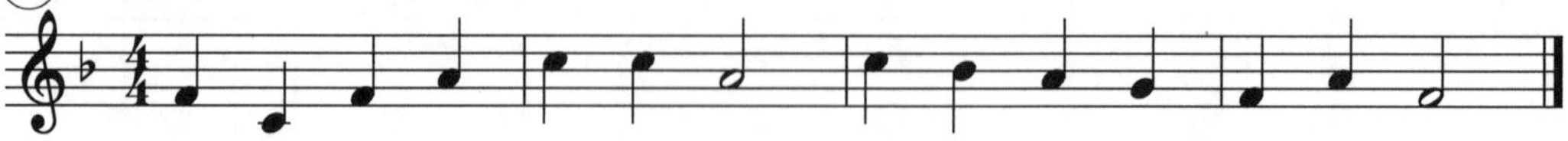

(9) p. 139

TENOR SIGHT READING TESTS

NAME ______________________________

DATE ______________________________

1 p. 14

2 p. 27

3 p. 46

4 p. 66

5 p. 84

6 p. 91

7 p. 100

8 p. 123

9 p. 139

BASS SIGHT READING TESTS

NAME ______________________________

DATE ______________________________

(1) p. 14

(2) p. 27

(3) p. 46

(4) p. 66

(5) p. 84

(6) p. 91

(7) p. 100

(8) p. 123

(9) p. 139

TREBLE SIGHT READING TESTS

NAME ______________________________

DATE ______________________________

(1) p. 14

(2) p. 24

(3) p. 36

(4) p. 57

(5) p. 92

(6) p. 115

(7) p. 122

(8) p. 154

(9) p. 171

(10) p. 186

TENOR SIGHT READING TESTS

NAME ______________________________

DATE ______________________________

(1) p. 14

(2) p. 24

(3) p. 36

(4) p. 57

(5) p. 92

(6) p. 115

(7) p. 122

(8) p. 154

(9) p. 171

(10) p. 186

BASS SIGHT READING TESTS

NAME ______________________________

DATE ______________________________

1 p. 14

2 p. 24

3 p. 36

4 p. 57

5 p. 92

6 p. 115

7 p. 122

8 p. 154

9 p. 171

10 p. 186

TREBLE SIGHT READING TESTS

NAME ____________________

DATE ____________________

(1) p. 6 Minor

(2) p. 26 Interval Practice

(3) p. 57 Primary Chords

(4) p. 85 Categories of Harmony

(5) p. 94 Compound Meter

(6) p. 123 Triplets & Duplets

(7) p. 140 Accidentals

(8) p. 173 Modulation

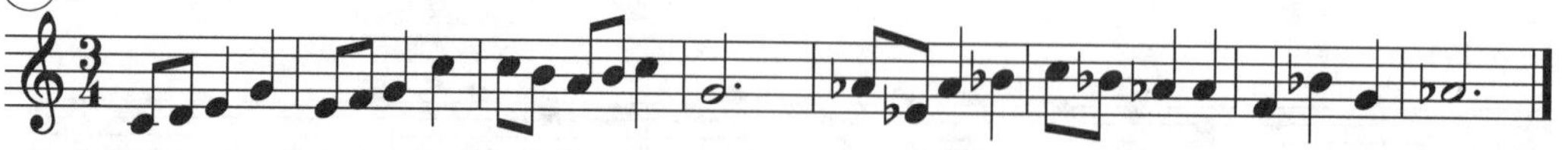

(9) p. 200 Dorian Mode

TENOR SIGHT READING TESTS

NAME ____________________________________

DATE ____________________________________

(1) p. 6 Minor

(2) p. 26 Interval Practice

(3) p. 57 Primary Chords

(4) p. 85 Categories of Harmony

(5) p. 94 Compound Meter

(6) p. 123 Triplets & Duplets

(7) p. 140 Accidentals

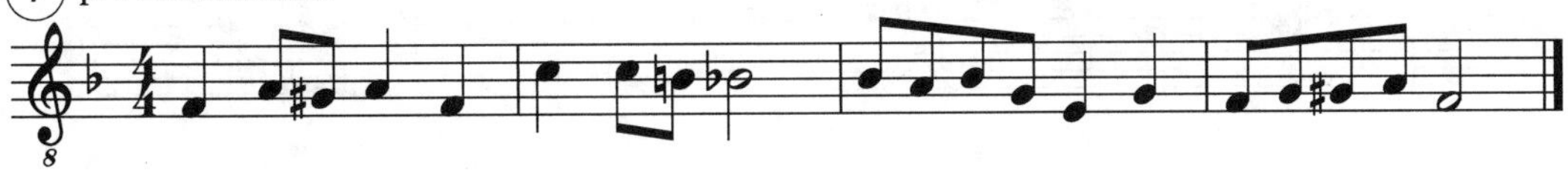

(8) p. 173 Modulation

(9) p. 200 Dorian Mode

BASS SIGHT READING TESTS

NAME ______________________________

DATE ______________________________

(1) p. 6 Minor

(2) p. 26 Interval Practice

(3) p. 57 Primary Chords

(4) p. 85 Categories of Harmony

(5) p. 94 Compound Meter

(6) p. 123 Triplets & Duplets

(7) p. 140 Accidentals

(8) p. 173 Modulation

(9) p. 200 Dorian Mode

CHECK YOUR RHYTHM

NAME ____________________

DATE ____________________

(1) p. 14

(2) p. 25

(3) p. 32

(4) p. 41

(5) p. 68

(6) p. 75

(7) p. 93

(8) p. 102

CHECK YOUR RHYTHM

NAME ______________________________

DATE ______________________________

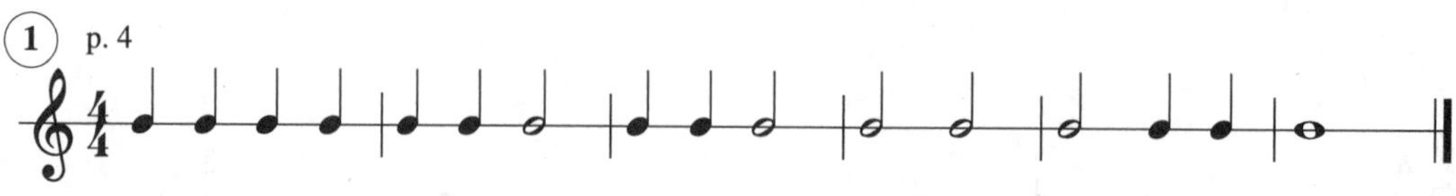

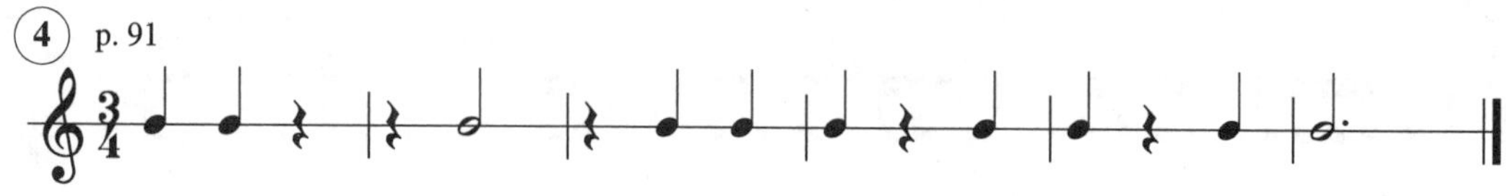

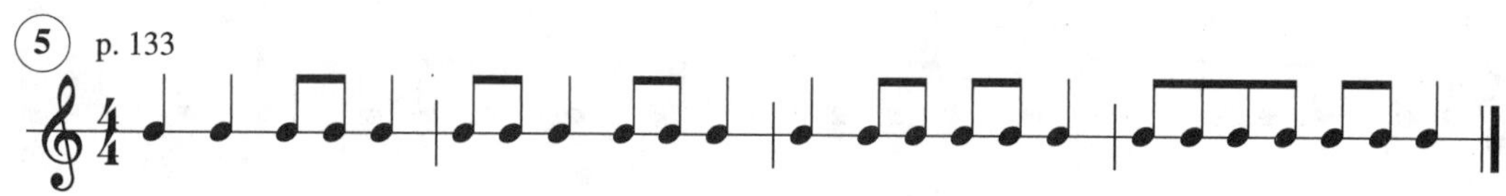

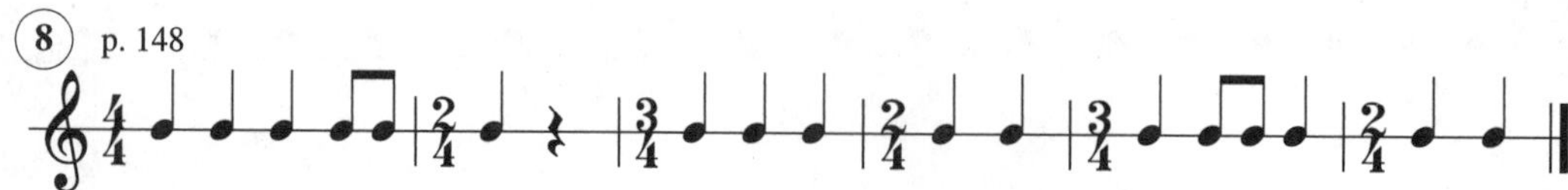

CHECK YOUR RHYTHM

NAME ____________________

DATE ____________________

(1) p. 4

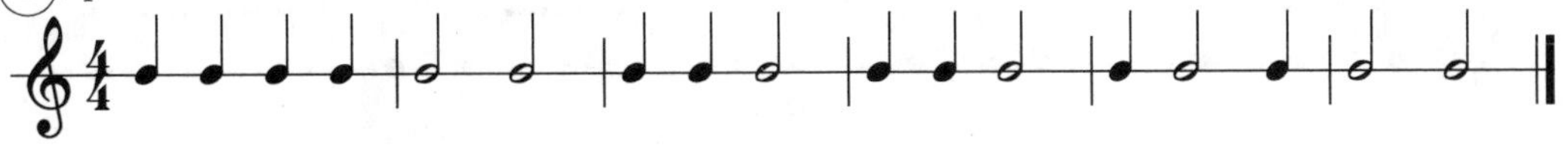

(2a) p. 11 (2b)

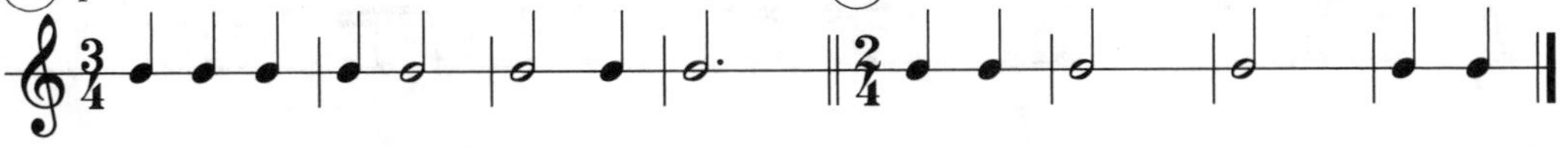

(3) p. 56

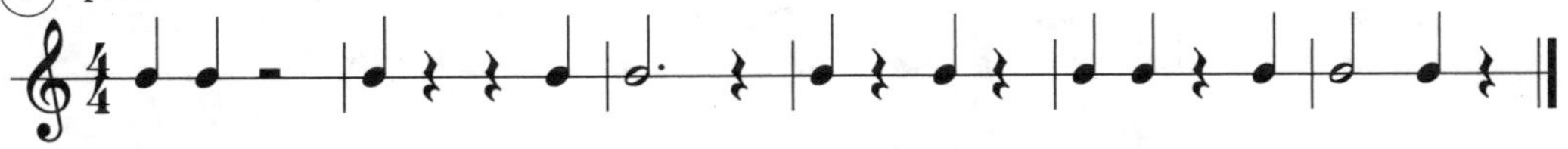

(4) p. 87

(5) p. 147

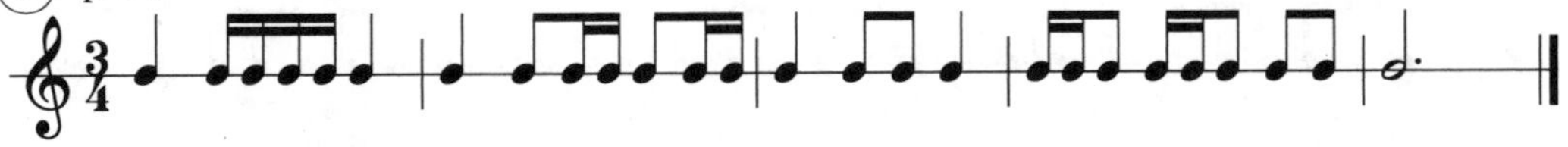

(6) p. 194

(7) p. 196

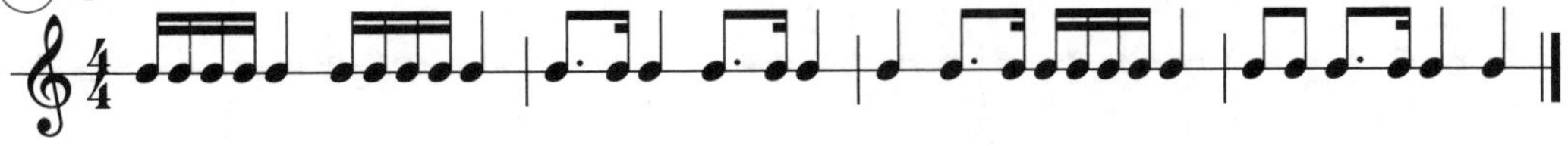

(8) p. 196

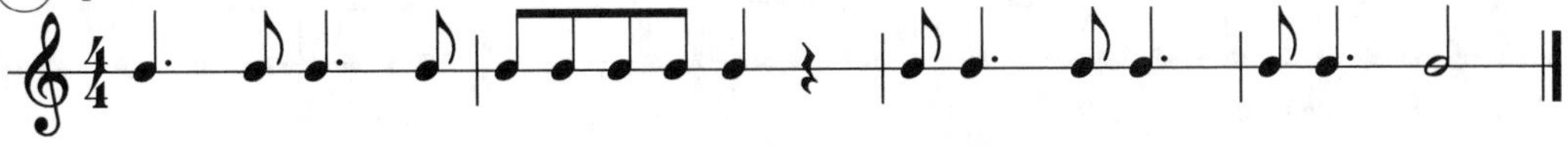

CHECK YOUR RHYTHM

NAME ______________________________

DATE ______________________________

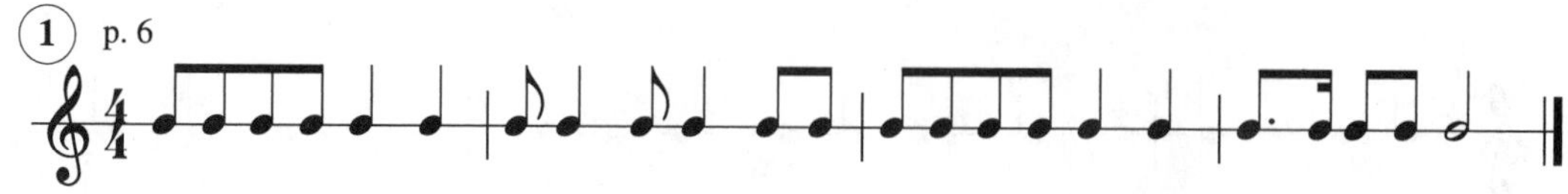

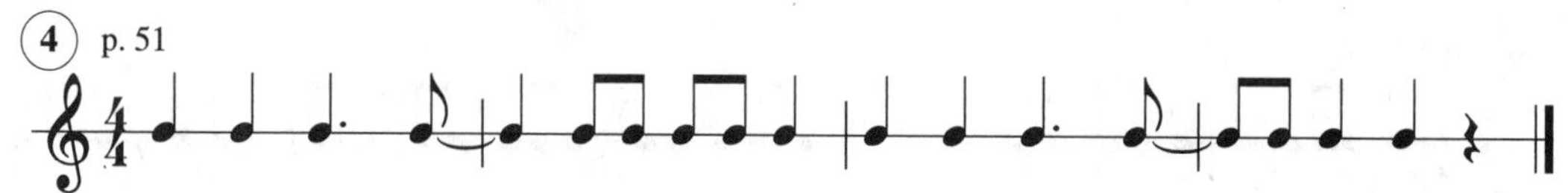

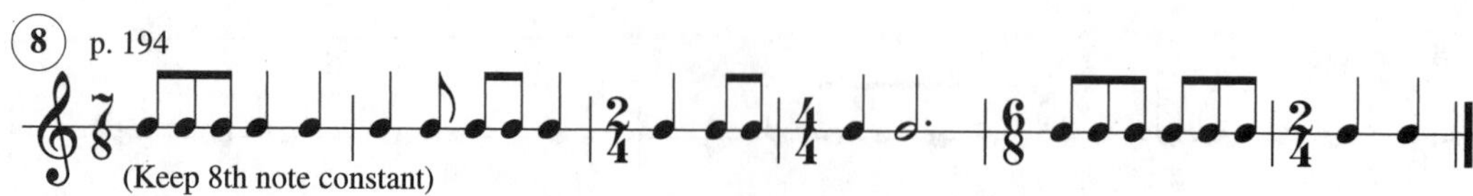

PERFORMANCE ASSESSMENT

- **Rehearsal Techniques**
- **Performance Evaluation**
- **Concert Etiquette**

TONE QUALITY - PART 1

NAME ______________________________

DATE ______________________________

Tone Quality (also known as TIMBRE) describes the sound a particular pitch makes. A voice, a clarinet and a trumpet may play exactly the same pitch, but you can hear the differences between them because they each have different timbres. It is easy to hear differences in tone quality, but those differences can be very difficult to describe in words. This checklist is designed to help you acquire a vocabulary to use when discussing tone quality.

Directions: Listen to a tape of yourself singing a familiar song and analyze your tone quality by marking an X on each line indicating how closely your tone comes to the descriptors on each line.

Example: A rather breathy singer might mark the first example as:

Breathy______X______________________________Clear

TONE QUALITY DESCRIPTORS

Breathy______________________________Clear

Rich______________________________Weak

Strong______________________________Weak

Loud______________________________Soft

Pleasant______________________________Unpleasant

Easily produced sound______________________________Harsh sound

On Pitch______________________________Off Pitch

Add your own descriptors:

Another way to use this checklist is to listen to a tape of your choir singing a familiar song and analyze the choir's tone quality by marking an X on each line indicating how closely the ensemble's tone comes to the descriptors on each line.

TONE QUALITY - PART 2

NAME ______________________________

DATE ______________________________

Tone Quality (also known as TIMBRE) describes the sound a particular pitch makes. A voice, a clarinet and a trumpet may play exactly the same pitch, but you can hear the differences between them because they each have different timbres. It is easy to hear differences in tone quality, but those differences can be very difficult to describe in words. This checklist is designed to help you acquire a vocabulary to use when discussing tone quality.

Directions: Listen to a tape of yourself singing a familiar song and analyze your tone quality by marking an X on each line indicating how closely your tone comes to the descriptors on each line.

Example: A singer with a thin tone would mark the first example as:

Resonant ______________________X________ Thin

TONE QUALITY DESCRIPTORS

Resonant	______________________	Thin
Warm	______________________	Cold, impersonal
Vibrato	______________________	No vibrato (straight tone)
Pleasant vibrato	______________________	Too wide vibrato
Pleasant vibrato	______________________	Too fast vibrato
Attack with straight tone, but end with vibrato	______________________	Even vibrato throughout each pitch
Accurately held pitch	______________________	Sliding to held pitch
Center of the pitch attacks	______________________	Scooping attacks
Pitches held evenly	______________________	Sliding down at ends of pitch
Flexibility in moving note to note	______________________	Difficulty in moving note to note
Easily initiating vowel sounds	______________________	Hard attack on vowel sounds

Another way to use this checklist is to listen to a tape of your choir singing a familiar song and analyze the choir's tone quality by marking an X on each line indicating how closely the ensemble's tone comes to the descriptors on each line.

BALANCE AND BLEND - PART 1

NAME ______________________________

DATE ______________________________

Balance refers to the loudness or softness of individual sections as compared to the other sections of the choir. Depending upon the song, a choir in which the soprano section sings louder than the others might be said to have a balance problem.

Blend refers to how alike the individual singers within a choir sound. No single voice is heard above the others. Blend problems might be due to singing too loudly, singing with non-uniform vowels, or using tone quality which does not match the rest of the group. Ideally, a well-blended choir sounds like one voice only stronger.

You are usually a member of which section? Soprano Alto Tenor Bass

TEST YOUR KNOWLEDGE

1. T F Balance might refer to how loud sopranos are in comparison to the rest of the choir.

2. T F Balance might refer to how loud basses are in comparison to the rest of the choir.

3. T F If one section is using a tone quality which does not match the rest of the group, the choir may be said to have a problem with blend.

4. T F If an individual singer's tone quality does not match the rest of the section, that section may be said to have a blend problem.

APPLY YOUR KNOWLEDGE

Listen to an audiotape of your choir singing a song they know very well. Analyze it carefully for correct balance and correct blend. Write your analysis in the space provided below.

Balance:

____

____

____

____

Blend:

____

____

____

____

BALANCE AND BLEND - PART 2

NAME ______________________________

DATE ______________________________

Balance refers to the loudness or softness of individual sections as compared to the other sections of the choir. Depending upon the song, a choir in which the soprano section sings louder than the others might be said to have a balance problem.

Blend refers to how alike the individual singers within a choir sound. No single voice is heard above the others. Blend problems might be due to singing too loudly, singing with non-uniform vowels, or using tone quality which does not match the rest of the group. Ideally, a well-blended choir sounds like one voice only stronger.

You are usually a member of which section? Soprano Alto Tenor Bass

BLEND AND BALANCE EXTENSION ACTIVITY

1. We know that balance refers to the loudness of individual sections in comparison to the other sections of the choir. But are there exceptions? Is balance always a matter of equal loudness among sections? Discuss situations in which a section might deliberately want to sing louder than the other sections. Find spots in your current pieces in which one section might sing louder than another. How would you define correct balance in this situation?

2. Are there circumstances in which an individual singer might want to sing louder than the ones around him or her? If so, identify places in your current pieces in which this might be true. How might proper blend be defined in this situation?

DICTION • LANGUAGES

NAME ______________________________

DATE ______________________________

Directions: Listen to a tape of yourself or your choir singing a familiar song and analyze your diction or the diction of your ensemble using the following checklist.

DICTION • LANGUAGE CHECKLIST (BASIC LEVEL)

_____ 1. Tall vowels are sung throughout the piece.

_____ 2. Beginnings of words can be clearly heard and understood.

_____ 3. Endings of words can be clearly heard and understood.

_____ 4. All words were clearly understood.

_____ 5. Foreign languages (if present) are correctly pronounced.

Identify one area on which you or your choir need(s) to work the most to improve diction.

DICTION • LANGUAGE CHECKLIST (ADVANCED LEVEL)

_____ 1. Diphthongs are sung correctly.

_____ 2. Crisp articulation of consonants is heard (explode the consonant and go to the vowel).

_____ 3. Word stress is appropriate. All syllables are not given the identical weight.

_____ 4. Foreign languages sound convincing (communicate something rather than just pronounce meaningless syllables).

Identify one area on which you or your choir need(s) to work the most to improve diction.

INTERPRETATION

NAME ______________________________

DATE ______________________________

Directions: Listen to a tape of your choir singing a familiar song and analyze the interpretation techniques of your choir. It would be helpful to follow along in your music as you listen to the tape.

Title of song: ______________________________

1. Yes No Dynamic contrasts were present.

2. Yes No Did the dynamics of your performance follow the intent of the composer?

3. Describe a specific example in the performance that caused you to answer #2 as you did.

____

____

____

____

4. Specify where in the music that more dynamic contrast could be used to make the song even more expressive and interesting.

____

____

____

____

5. Yes No Were longer or held notes sung expressively? (gradually louder or softer, or with a rise and fall in dynamics)

6. Describe a specific example in the performance that caused you to answer #5 as you did.

____

7. Identify a single musical phrase in the music that, in your opinion, was expressively sung. What expressive characteristics did you hear in that phrase?

____

____

____

____

8. Interpretation Extension Activity
With your director's permission, direct or conduct your ensemble in an expressive performance of a familiar song. Reflect on how you made the song more expressive.

ENSEMBLE PRECISION

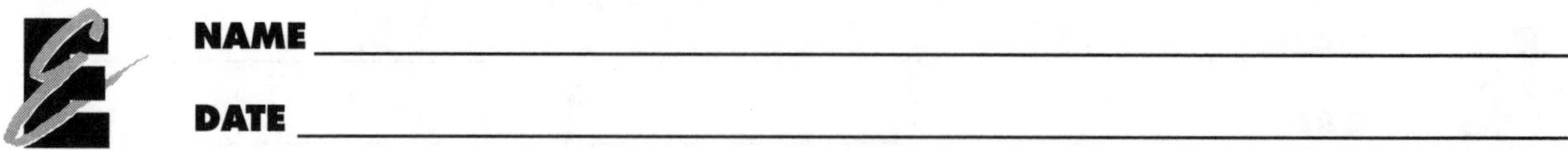

NAME ____________________

DATE ____________________

Precision in choral singing has to do with all singers being precise and exacting in rhythms, diction (vowels and consonants), attacks and releases (starting and ending of words), and correct pitches.

Directions: Listen to an audio performance of a song performed by your choir. To analyze the precision of your ensemble, complete the following. List specific words, pages and measures which need improvement in precision.

Title of song: ____________________

Ensemble Precision	Specific Word	Page	Measure
1. All consonant attacks precisely together except in the following:			
2. All consonant releases (endings precisely together) except in the following:			
3. All vowel attacks precisely together except in the following:			
4. All rhythms performed accurately and exactly together except in the following:			
5. All vowels pronounced uniformly except in the following:			
6. All pitches are sung accurately except in the following:			

PHYSICAL INVOLVEMENT • ATTENTIVENESS

NAME ____________________

DATE ____________________

Excellent choirs have singers which look and act involved in the music!

Directions: View a video of your choir singing. Analyze the physical involvement of your choir by using this checklist.

1. Facial Expression (circle any which apply)

Animated	Happy	Pleasant
Silly	Sorrowful	Bored
Stayed the same	Varied facial expressions	Serious

Your own descriptor:

How appropriate was the facial expression to the style and meaning of this song?
Very appropriate 1 2 3 4 5 Not at all appropriate

2. Eye Motions (circle any which apply)

Open and alert	Almost closed	Looked bored
Never changing	Lots of variety in eye motions	Could not see eyes
Looked down continuously		

Your own descriptor:

How appropriate was the facial expression to the style and meaning of this song?
Very appropriate 1 2 3 4 5 Not at all appropriate

3. Physical Movement (circle any which apply)

Bounced too much	Distracting movement	Hands at sides
Hands in pockets	Hands pulling at clothing	Tapped foot
No changes in motion	Swayed slightly	Stiff and wooden
Slouched	Good posture	Weight on both feet

No obvious motion, but seemed involved in the music

Your own descriptor:

How appropriate was the facial expression to the style and meaning of this song?
Very appropriate 1 2 3 4 5 Not at all appropriate

4. Attentiveness (circle any which apply)

Watched conductor at all times	Eyes wandered around the room
Seemed aware of changes in the music	Head was in the music
Seemed unaware of any changes in the music	

Your own descriptor:

How appropriate was the facial expression to the style and meaning of this song?
Very appropriate 1 2 3 4 5 Not at all appropriate

ATTENTIVENESS • BEHAVIOR EXPECTATIONS

NAME ______________________________

DATE ______________________________

Remember: You should improve as a singer by being a part of the choir and the choir should improve because of you being a part of it. Always find ways to contribute!

Directions: Check yourself on attentiveness during rehearsals using the following checklist.

1. Always come to choir prepared. List items you need for class.
   - Ⓐ music
   - Ⓑ positive attitude
   - Ⓒ ____________________
   - Ⓓ ____________________

2. Always come to choir on time and ready to sing. Check items showing readiness for class.
   - ____ In place when the bell rings
   - ____ Running down the hall as the bell rings
   - ____ Asking to borrow a pencil as the bell rings

3. Always come to choir with a positive attitude. Check items showing positive attitude.
   - ____ Leave your troubles at the door. Sing.
   - ____ Bad attitudes are contagious. Don't spread yours around.
   - ____ Act cheerful even if you have to fake it occasionally.

4. Avoid talking during rehearsal. List things you could do besides talk while another section is rehearsing.
   - Ⓐ study your own part
   - Ⓑ ____________________
   - Ⓒ ____________________

5. Watch your director at all times while singing. List reasons why watching the director is important:
   - Ⓐ director keeps the group together
   - Ⓑ ____________________
   - Ⓒ ____________________

6. Respect the efforts of others. Check items which show respect for others.
   - ____ Laugh when someone sings.
   - ____ Listen attentively while someone sings.
   - ____ Tell the person they did well.
   - ____ Talk while others are singing.

   Your own suggestions:

7. Be a leader in choir. Check items which show leadership.
   - ____ Be a role model of attentiveness during choir.
   - ____ Be willing to try new things your director suggests.
   - ____ Talk during rehearsals.
   - ____ Offer to help a person with his/her music or sight-reading.
   - ____ Use good singing posture without director's reminder.
   - ____ Share your hand lotion with other choir members during class.

   Your own suggestions:

ESSAY FOLLOWING A FORMAL CHORAL PERFORMANCE

NAME ____

DATE ____

Directions: Answer the following questions in essay form using one paragraph per question. Please write with complete sentences and be prepared to discuss your ideas in class.

Concert ____________________________ Date of Concert ____________________________

1. Musically speaking, what was the strongest song or portion of the program. Why?

2. Musically speaking, what was the weakest song or portion of the program. Why?

3. Musically speaking, what did you enjoy most about the concert?

4. Share comments your parents, friends or teachers made about the concert.

ESSAY FOLLOWING A COMMUNITY PERFORMANCE

NAME ____________________

DATE ____________________

Directions: Answer the following questions in essay form using one paragraph per question. Please write with complete sentences and be prepared to discuss your ideas in class.

Concert ____________________ Date of Concert ____________________

1. What positive comments do you have to share about the concert?
2. Musically speaking, in what areas does our choir need the most improvement?
3. What suggestions do you have to improve the trip (concert), if we do it again?
4. In what ways, if any, did this concert contribute to the community?

MEANING OF TEXT

NAME ______________________________

DATE ______________________________

Directions: Study the text of the assigned song. Read through it several times for understanding. Look up the definitions of any words you do not understand. Then write an introduction to the song which will serve as an explanation of the meaning of the text. Use your own words in writing the introduction and express the text in modern terms.

Title of Song ______________________________

Poet (lyricist) ______________________________

Your introduction to the song explaining the meaning of the text.

SEMESTER ESSAY EXAM

NAME ______________________________

DATE ______________________________

Directions: During the semester you have been actively involved in choir with class work, rehearsals, and performances. In your opinion, what have you learned specifically in the following areas? On your own paper, write your answers in essay form using complete sentences and correct spelling.

1. The physical aspects of good singing (posture, breathing, mouth position, etc.)
   What learned
   Specific example

2. Music reading (rhythmic and melodic)
   What learned
   Specific example

3. The art of public performance (stage presence)
   What learned
   Specific example

4. The artistic demands of good performance (interpretation)
   What learned
   Specific example

5. Teamwork and cooperation
   What learned
   Specific example

6. Other things you have learned in choir this semester
   What learned
   Specific example

BASIC PERFORMANCE CHECKLIST

NAME ________________________________

DATE ________________________________

Concert Title: ______________________________ Concert Date: ____________________

This evaluation is based on: _____ my reflection or memory of the concert
_____ video tape of concert ____ audio tape of concert

Directions: Fill in the chart ranking the choir's overall performance with 1 being the weakest ranking and 5 being the strongest for each element. Then decide which song in the concert demonstrated the best example of the element and then the song which demonstrated least well the element of performance.

Element of Performance	Overall Ranking	Most effective – title of song	Least effective – title of song
Dynamic Contrast	1 2 3 4 5		
Tall, uniform vowels	1 2 3 4 5		
Attacks precise	1 2 3 4 5		
Consonant endings precise	1 2 3 4 5		
Accurate rhythm	1 2 3 4 5		
Accurate pitches	1 2 3 4 5		
Good tone quality	1 2 3 4 5		
Good stage presence	1 2 3 4 5		

Identify two areas than need the most improvement before the next concert. Work hard to show improvement in these areas.

1. ______________________________ 2. ______________________________

ADVANCED PERFORMANCE CHECKLIST

NAME ____________________

DATE ____________________

Concert Title: ____________________ Concert Date: ____________________

This evaluation is based on: _____ my reflection or memory of the concert
_____ video tape of concert _____ audio tape of concert

Directions: Fill in the chart ranking the choir's overall performance with 1 being the weakest ranking and 5 being the strongest for each element. Then decide which song in the concert demonstrated the best example of the element and then the song which demonstrated least well the element of performance.

Element of Performance	Overall Ranking	Most effective – title of song	Least effective – title of song
Interpretation/Musicality	1 2 3 4 5		
Ensemble Precision	1 2 3 4 5		
Tone Quality	1 2 3 4 5		
Blend	1 2 3 4 5		
Balance	1 2 3 4 5		
Stage Presence	1 2 3 4 5		
Audience Response	1 2 3 4 5		

Identify two areas than need the most improvement before the next concert. Work hard to show improvement in these areas.

1. ____________________ 2. ____________________

CONCERT ETIQUETTE

NAME ______________________________

DATE ______________________________

Whether you are attending the opera, the ballet, a theater production, the marching band half time show, a rock concert, or a formal musical concert, specific guidelines dictate appropriate behavior for each particular event. Understanding the common courtesies involved for each different event allows everyone involved, including both performers and the audience, to enjoy the performance.

While the different activities do share some common basic behavior expectations, certain courtesies are unique to specific events. It is important for us as audience members to be aware of these differences and behave in a manner that gives thoughtful consideration and respect to everyone involved. Let's look at some basic behavior guidelines that are appropriate for formal musical concerts.

- Plan to arrive on time. If you do arrive after the performance has begun, wait outside the auditorium until a break between selections (the audience is clapping) to enter the concert hall.
- While you never want to leave during a concert performance, emergencies do sometimes occur. If at all possible, wait to exit the hall until a break in the performance or until a place where it will not interfere with the overall performance.
- Talking or rustling around during a performance keeps others in the audience from both hearing and enjoying the particular event they have chosen to attend. Such activities can also distract the performers, interfering with their concentration.
- Take your cue from the performers or from the conductor when it comes to singing along or keeping time by clapping or stamping the feet. It is usually best to wait for an invitation for such audience participation.
- As a courtesy to the performers as well as to other audience members, cellular telephones should remain off during any performance. If you must wear a beeper, make sure it is set so no audible sound will be heard.
- When young children attend formal concerts, they learn to be good audience participants. Crying, chattering and otherwise noisy children, however, should be removed from a performance immediately and should return only if such behavior does not recur.
- If an episode of coughing becomes prolonged, it is advisable to leave the performance, returning after the coughing has stopped at a time that is not disruptive to others in the audience.
- Applause is what affirms to the performers that the audience is enjoying and appreciative of their efforts. The conductor and any guest soloists are applauded when they walk onto the stage. Applause for the music is held until the end of each selection or until the end of the entire performance, when the conductor turns toward the audience and bows.
- Catcalls, whistling, or other loud audible noises are best reserved for athletic events or other activities that elicit exuberant responses from audience members and are never appropriate at formal concerts.

CONCERT ETIQUETTE QUIZ, BASIC

NAME ______________________________

DATE ______________________________

Indicate in the blank whether each statement is True (T) or False (F).

_____ 1. Whistling and calling out are appropriate behavior at a formal concert.

_____ 2. Specific guidelines dictate appropriate behavior at different events.

_____ 3. If you arrive late for a performance, just go immediately to your seat.

_____ 4. Talking and rustling around during a performance can distract the performers on the stage.

_____ 5. It is acceptable to simply hope that a crying child will stop at sometime during a performance.

_____ 6. Beepers should be set so that no audible sound can be heard during a performance.

_____ 7. If you feel the urge to clap or sing along during a performance, go ahead and chime right in.

_____ 8. Consideration and respect for everyone involved in a performance should be the ultimate goal.

_____ 9. Applause should begin before the conductor has given the final cut off.

_____10. It is best to leave cellular telephones turned off during a performance.

List three appropriate behaviors you feel are most important to remember when attending a formal musical concert.

11. ______________________________

12. ______________________________

13. ______________________________

CONCERT ETIQUETTE QUIZ, ADVANCED

NAME ______________________________

DATE ______________________________

Circle the letter of the best answer in each statement.

1. It is appropriate to leave a performance at all but which of the following times
   A. If a child is crying or being otherwise noisy and disruptive.
   B. At the end of the performance.
   C. During a song that you don't particularly care for.
   D. You have a prolonged coughing episode.

2. If you arrive late for a performance, it is most appropriate to
   A. Hurry immediately to your seat regardless of what is occurring on stage.
   B. Open the auditorium doors so that you can check it out.
   C. Go right in during the middle of a musical selection.
   D. Wait outside the auditorium until a break between selections and you hear the audience begin to clap.

3. Applause is appropriate at all but which of the following times
   A. At the end of a concert performance.
   B. When the conductor walks onto the stage.
   C. At the completion of an individual musical selection.
   D. In the middle of a song.

4. Why is it important for audience members to be aware of appropriate etiquette expectations?

5. Think about which inappropriate audience behaviors are most distracting to you as a performer. Discuss appropriate ways for a performer to deal with these behaviors.

6. Based on what you have learned about appropriate concert etiquette, what can <u>you</u> do to become a better audience member?

MUSIC HISTORY

- **Medieval Era**
- **Renaissance Era**
- **Baroque Era**
- **Classical Era**
- **Romantic Era**
- **Contemporary Era**

THE MIDDLE AGES

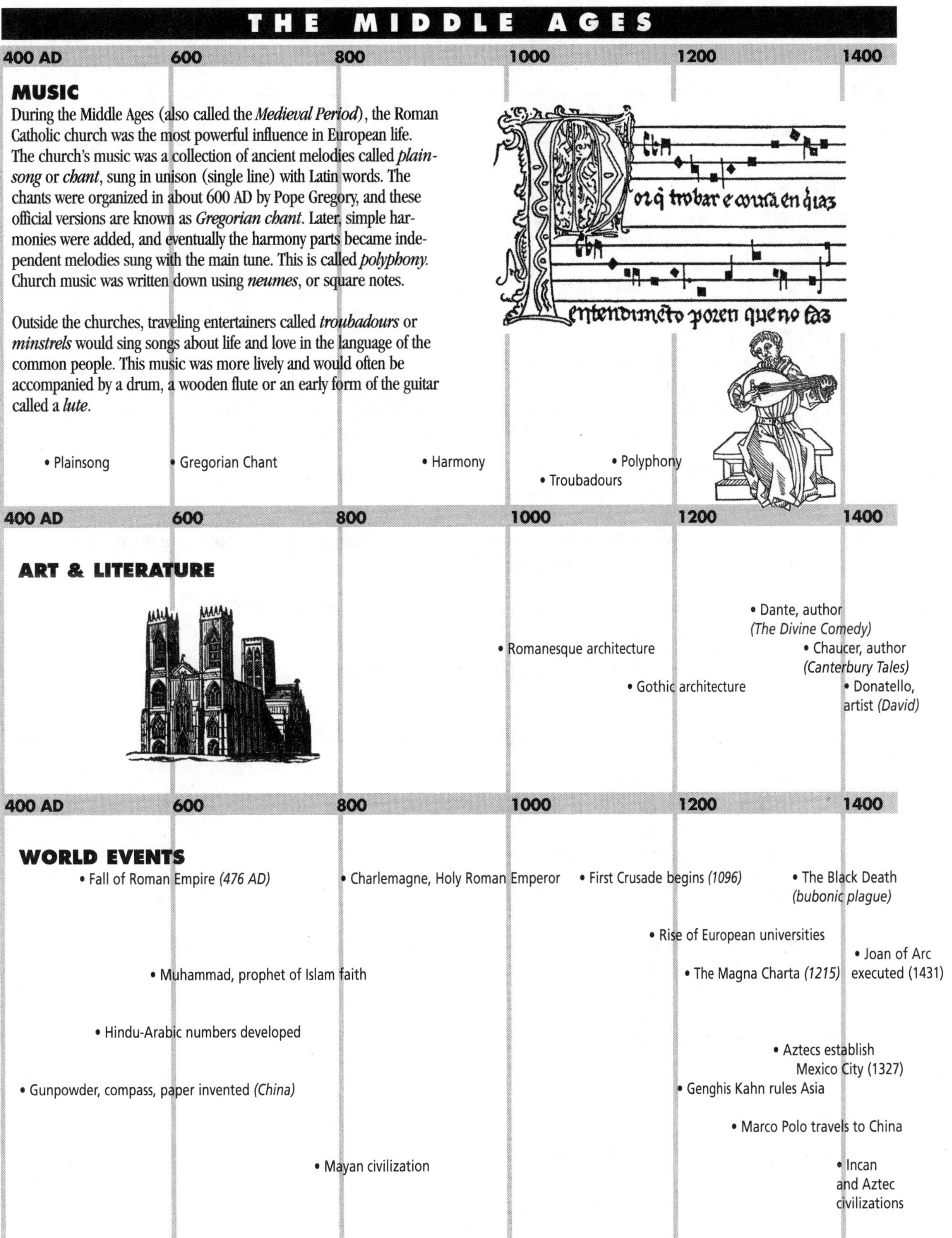

400 AD | 600 | 800 | 1000 | 1200 | 1400

MUSIC

During the Middle Ages (also called the *Medieval Period*), the Roman Catholic church was the most powerful influence in European life. The church's music was a collection of ancient melodies called *plainsong* or *chant*, sung in unison (single line) with Latin words. The chants were organized in about 600 AD by Pope Gregory, and these official versions are known as *Gregorian chant*. Later, simple harmonies were added, and eventually the harmony parts became independent melodies sung with the main tune. This is called *polyphony*. Church music was written down using *neumes*, or square notes.

Outside the churches, traveling entertainers called *troubadours* or *minstrels* would sing songs about life and love in the language of the common people. This music was more lively and would often be accompanied by a drum, a wooden flute or an early form of the guitar called a *lute*.

- Plainsong
- Gregorian Chant
- Harmony
- Troubadours
- Polyphony

400 AD | 600 | 800 | 1000 | 1200 | 1400

ART & LITERATURE

- Romanesque architecture
- Gothic architecture
- Dante, author *(The Divine Comedy)*
- Chaucer, author *(Canterbury Tales)*
- Donatello, artist *(David)*

400 AD | 600 | 800 | 1000 | 1200 | 1400

WORLD EVENTS

- Gunpowder, compass, paper invented *(China)*
- Fall of Roman Empire *(476 AD)*
- Hindu-Arabic numbers developed
- Muhammad, prophet of Islam faith
- Mayan civilization
- Charlemagne, Holy Roman Emperor
- First Crusade begins *(1096)*
- Rise of European universities
- The Magna Charta *(1215)*
- Genghis Kahn rules Asia
- Marco Polo travels to China
- Aztecs establish Mexico City (1327)
- The Black Death *(bubonic plague)*
- Joan of Arc executed (1431)
- Incan and Aztec civilizations

MIDDLE AGES (MEDIEVAL ERA) 400-1450

NAME ______________________________

DATE ______________________________

Typical Characteristics of Medieval Music
- A cappella music (voices without accompaniment) was prevalent.
- The most common sacred (religious) music was the mass (order of the Catholic service).
- Sacred music texts were written in Latin.
- Sacred music, even after harmony developed, was based on Gregorian chant.
- Common secular (non-religious) vocal forms were accompanied by lute, pipe, drums, and other instruments of the day.
- Dynamic changes were very subdued.
- Chant was monophonic ("one sound" or a single line of music with no harmony).
- Music in the late Middle Ages became polyphonic ("many songs" or two or more melodies combined). The rise of polyphony was actually the beginning of harmony as we know it.

Listening Selection: *Alma Redemptoris Mater* by Palestrina (Renaissance)
Glorificamus te by Butler (Contemporary)

Directions: Although these two selections are not from the medieval era, they both use monophonic medieval era chants. Answer the following questions.

1. An example of monophonic chant occurs where in *Alma Redemptoris Mater?*
   Beginning Middle End

2. An example of monophonic chant occurs where in *Glorificamus te?*
   Beginning Middle End

3. Listen closely to *Glorificamus te.* Which of the characteristics below would indicate that this piece was not written during the Middle Ages?
   _____ Piano accompaniment
   _____ Very rhythmic, non-subdued accompaniment
   _____ Much dynamic contrast
   _____ Unison, monophonic singing
   _____ Complex rhythms
   _____ Latin text

4. Listen closely to *Alma Redemptoris Mater.* Which of the characteristics below would indicate that this piece was not written during the Middle Ages?
   _____ Piano accompaniment
   _____ Complicated harmonies
   _____ Some dynamic contrast
   _____ Unison, monophonic singing
   _____ Complex rhythms
   _____ Latin text

5. Why do you think a composer would choose to use a style hundreds of years old?

MIDDLE AGES (MEDIEVAL ERA) QUIZ

NAME ______________________________

DATE ______________________________

1. The Middle Ages were also known as
   A. the Twentieth Century
   B. the Medieval Period
   C. the Romantic Era

2. Gregorian chants were organized by
   A. Pope *Gregory*
   B. Pope John
   C. Pope Paul

3. Church music was written down using neumes, where notes were shaped like
   A. triangles
   B. circles
   C. squares

4. A form of music in which there is "one sound" or a single line of music, with no harmony is referred to as
   A. polyphonic
   B. polyester
   C. monophonic

5. A famous book written during the Middle Ages is
   A. *Canterbury Tales*
   B. *Alice in Wonderland*
   C. *Little Women*

6. Name three world events that happened during this time period.
   -
   -
   -

7. Write a paragraph about what you think life would have been like in the Middle Ages.

THE RENAISSANCE

1450 | 1500 | 1550 | 1600

MUSIC

The era from about 1450–1600 was featured in the halls of the nobility. Two entertaining forms of secular songs were the madrigal and the villancico, sung by 4 or 5 voices at many special occasions. Instrumental music became popular as new string, brass and woodwind instruments were developed.

A form of church music was the motet, with 3 or 4 independent vocal parts. New forms of church music developed. In the new protestant churches, the entire congregation sang chorales: simple HARMONIZED melodies in even rhythms like the hymns we hear today. Important Renaissance composers were:

- Josquin des Prez (c. 1450-1521) *Tu pauperum refugium*
- Giovanni da Palestrina (c. 1529-1594) *Alma redemptoris mater*
- Orlando di Lasso (c. 1532-1594) *Tutto lo di mi dici "Canta"*
- Tomas Luis de Victoria (c. 1549-1611) *Vere languores*
- Giovanni Giacomo Gastoldi (c. 1550-1622) *Poi ch'el mio foco e spento*
- Thomas Weelkes (c. 1575-1623) *In Pride of May*
- Protestant church music
- First printed music
- Madrigals

1450 | 1500 | 1550 | 1600

ART & LITERATURE

- Leonardo da Vinci, scientist/artist *(Mona Lisa, The Last Supper)*
- Michelangelo, artist *(Sistine Chapel, David)*
- Machiavelli, author *(The Prince)*

- Shakespeare, author *(Romeo and Juliet, Hamlet)*

1450 | 1500 | 1550 | 1600

WORLD EVENTS

- Gutenberg invents printing press *(1454)*
- Martin Luther ignites Protestant Reformation *(1517)*
- Columbus travels to America *(1492)*
- Magellan circles globe *(1519)*
- Copernicus begins modern astronomy *(1543)*
- First European contact with Japan *(1549)*
- Elizabeth I becomes Queen of England *(1558)*

RENAISSANCE ERA 1450-1600

NAME ______________________________

DATE ______________________________

Typical Characteristics of Renaissance Music

- A cappella vocal music is still the norm.
- Sacred music forms include the Latin mass and motet.
- Much sacred music is built on pre-existing melodies (usually chants).
- Sacred vocal music begins to be written in the language that the people speak (vernacular) instead of exclusively in Latin.
- Secular vocal music includes English madrigal, Italian villancico, French chanson.
- Instrumental forms are developing (usually derived from dance music).
- Instruments remain unspecified. (Composer does not indicate which instrument plays which part)

Listening Selection: *Alma Redemptoris Mater* by Palestrina (ca. 1525-1594)

Directions: Listen to the recording and answer the following questions.

1. Based on your perceptive listening, circle the Renaissance characteristics which are present in *Alma Redemptoris Mater*. Note: Do not circle every Renaissance characteristic, only the ones you can hear.

   A cappella
   Secular text
   Vernacular text
   Example of madrigal, villancico or chanson
   Instrumental accompaniment
   Sacred text
   Latin text

2. Based on your listening, check all true statements:

   _____ Sounds mostly hymn-like (all parts moving together/same words at same time)
   _____ Sounds like a piece sung by women
   _____ Sounds like a piece sung by men and women
   _____ Accompaniment uses typical Renaissance instruments (lute, etc.)
   _____ Sounds like it may be Latin
   _____ Sounds like a secular madrigal, villancico or chanson

3. How would you describe the mood or general feeling of this piece? Why do you think that mood might be characteristic of a Renaissance piece?
   - Mood

   - Why characteristic?

RENAISSANCE ERA QUIZ

NAME ____________________

DATE ____________________

1. The Renaissance lasted from
   A. 1900-1925
   B. 1450-1600
   C. 1890-1900

2. The word "Renaissance" means
   A. recycle
   B. return
   C. rebirth

3. Non-religious music is called
   A. secular
   B. sacred
   C. symphony

4. Simple harmonized melodies in even rhythms like the hymns we hear today are called
   A. chants
   B. operas
   C. chorales

5. An important Renaissance composer was
   A. Franz Schubert
   B. Josquin des Prez
   C. John Williams

6. An important Renaissance invention that brought music to the homes of the middle class was
   A. the printing press
   B. MTV
   C. the radio

7. A famous painting by Leonardo da Vinci is
   A. Lisa Marie
   B. Mona Lisa
   C. Ramona Lee

8. Name three world events that occurred during the Renaissance.
   -
   -
   -

9. Extra credit: How would your life have been different if you had lived during the Renaissance instead of today?

THE BAROQUE ERA

1600 | 1650 | 1700 | 1750

MUSIC

Music and the arts (and even clothing) became fancier and more dramatic in the *Baroque* era (about 1600–1750). Like the fancy decorations of Baroque church architecture, melodies were often played with *grace notes*, or quick nearby tones added to decorate them. Rhythms became more complex with time signatures, bar lines and faster-moving melodic lines. Our now familiar major and minor scales formed the basis for harmony, and chords were standardized to what we often hear today.

The harpsichord became the most popular keyboard instrument, with players often *improvising* (making up) their parts using the composer's chords and bass line. Violin making reached new heights in Italy. Operas, ballets and small orchestras were beginning to take shape, as composers specified the exact instruments, tempos and dynamics to be performed.

- Henry Purcell *(1659–1695), Trumpet Voluntary, Trumpet Tune*
- Antonio Vivaldi *(1676–1741) Gloria*
- George Frideric Handel *(1685–1759), Messiah, Let the Whole Earth Stand in Awe*
- Johann Sebastian Bach *(1685–1750), Christmas Oratorio, Wachet Auf! Cantata No. 14*
- First public opera house *(Vienna, 1637)*
- Stradivarius violins *(1700–1737)*
- First piano built *(1709)*
- Dietrich Buxtehude *(1637-1707), Zion hört die Wächter singen*
- Alessandro Scarlatti *(1660-1725) Exultate Deo*

1600 | 1650 | 1700 | 1750

ART & LITERATURE

- Cervantes, author *(Don Quixote)*
- Milton, author *(Paradise Lost)*
- Defoe, author *(Robinson Crusoe)*
- Rubens, artist *(Descent from the Cross)*
- Kabuki theater in Japan
- Rembrandt, artist *(The Night Watch)*
- Swift, author *(Gulliver's Travels)*
- Taj Mahal built *(1634–1653)*

1600 | 1650 | 1700 | 1750

WORLD EVENTS

- Salem witchcraft trials *(1692)*
- Galileo identifies gravity *(1602)*
- Louis XIV builds Versailles Palace *(1661–1708)*
- First English colony in America *(Jamestown, 1607)*
- Quebec founded by Champlain *(1608)*
- First slaves to America *(1619)*
- Isaac Newton *(1642-1727)* formulates principals of physics and math

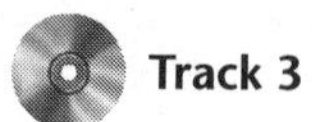

THE BAROQUE PERIOD 1600-1750

NAME ______________________________

DATE ______________________________

Typical Characteristics of Baroque Music

- Voice and instruments combined were common.
- A cappella music (voices without accompaniment) became less common.
- Common sacred (religious) vocal forms were cantata and oratorio.
- Common secular (non-religious) vocal forms were opera and cantata.
- Instruments were specified, rather than left to the choice of players.
- Major and minor tonality became common.
- Terraced dynamics (alternating loud and soft phrases instead of getting gradually louder or softer) became the preferred style.
- Continuously moving rhythms were common. The accompaniments would often contain repeated eighth notes.

Listening Selection: *Let the Whole Earth Stand in Awe* by Handel (1685-1759)

Directions: Listen to *Let the Whole Earth Stand in Awe* as many times as necessary to answer the following questions:

1. T F This work combines both voices and instruments.
2. T F This work is a cappella.
3. T F This work has a sacred text.
4. T F This work uses terraced dynamics.
5. T F This work uses gradually changing dynamics.

Extended Listening:
Listen closely to the accompaniment of *Let the Whole Earth Stand in Awe.* Do you think that this example has a continuously moving accompaniment? Explain why you chose this answer.

Enrichment Activities:
Listen to or sing other works from the Baroque time period. Analyze the Baroque characteristics of these works. Discuss which of the characteristics listed above appear in the piece. Famous works from the Baroque era include Handel's Messiah or his *Water Music Suite,* J. S. Bach's *Little Fugue in G Minor* or one of his *Brandenburg Concerti,* or *Vivaldi's Four Seasons.*

BAROQUE ERA QUIZ

NAME ______________________________

DATE ______________________________

1. The Baroque Era lasted from
   A. 1400-1500
   B. 1900-1950
   C. 1600-1750
2. The most popular keyboard instrument of the time was
   A. harpsichord
   B. synthesizer
   C. grand piano
3. Making up music using the composer's chords and bass line was called
   A. conducting
   B. improvising
   C. arranging
4. Quick nearby tones added to decorate melodies were called
   A. grace notes
   B. eighth notes
   C. instant notes
5. A famous violin-maker in Italy was
   A. Rubens
   B. Stradivarius
   C. Cervantes
6. A famous artist during the Baroque Era was
   A. Defoe
   B. Rembrandt
   C. Swift
7. Match the following music with the name of the composer.

_____ *Sound the Trumpet*	A. Johann Sebastian Bach
_____ *The Messiah*	B. Antonio Vivaldi
_____ *Gloria*	C. Henry Purcell
_____ *Christmas Oratorio*	D. George Frideric Handel

8. Name three world events that occurred during the Baroque Era.
   •
   •
   •
9. Extra credit: For what are the people in Questions 5 and 6 known?

THE CLASSICAL ERA

1750 | 1775 | 1800 | 1820

MUSIC

The *Classical* era, from about 1750 to the early 1800's, was a time of great contrasts. While patriots fought for the rights of the common people in the American and French revolutions, composers were employed to entertain wealthy nobles and aristocrats. Music became simpler and more elegant, with melodies often flowing over accompaniment patterns in regular 4-bar phrases. Like the architecture of ancient *Classical* Greece, music was fit together in "building blocks" by balancing one phrase against another, or one entire section against another.

The piano replaced the harpsichord and became the most popular instrument for the *concerto* (solo) with orchestra accompaniment. The string quartet became the favorite form of *chamber* (small group) music, and orchestra concerts featured *symphonies* (longer compositions with 4 contrasting parts or *movements*). Toward the end of this era, Beethoven's changing musical style led the way toward the more emotional and personal expression of Romantic music.

- Franz Josef Haydn *(1732–1809), Gloria from Heilegmesse, Achieved is Thy Glorious Work*
- Wolfgang Amadeus Mozart *(1756–1791), Ave Verum Corpus, Gloria in Excelsis from Twelfth Mass, Regina Angelorum*
- Ludwig van Beethoven *(1770–1827), Ode To Joy, theme from Violin Concerto, 5th Symphony, 9th Symphony*

1750 | 1775 | 1800 | 1820

ART & LITERATURE

- Samuel Johnson, author *(Dictionary)*
- Voltaire, author *(Candide)*
- Gainsborough, artist *(The Blue Boy)*
- *Encyclopedia Britannica*, first edition
- Wm. Wordsworth, author *(Lyrical Ballads)*
- Goethe, author *(Faust)*
- Goya, artist *(Witch's Sabbath)*
- Jane Austen, author *(Pride and Prejudice)*

1750 | 1775 | 1800 | 1820

WORLD EVENTS

- Ben Franklin discovers electricity *(1751)*
- American Revolution *(1775–1783)*
- French Revolution *(1789–1794)*
- Napoleon crowned Emperor of France *(1804)*
- Lewis and Clark explore northwest *(1804)*
- Metronome invented *(1815)*
- First steamship crosses Atlantic *(1819)*

CLASSICAL ERA 1750-1820

NAME ______________________

DATE ______________________

Typical Characteristics of Classical Music

- Balanced phrases (phrases usually the same length)
- Obvious cadences (stopping points in the music/musical punctuation)
- Tuneful, singable melodies
- Accompaniments underneath the melodies had regularly recurring accents.
- Symphony, solo concerto, string quartet and sonata were popular instrumental forms. All were works with multiple movements.
- Dynamic contrasts became subtler, not as sudden as in Baroque (few terraced dynamics).
- Expansion of orchestra into four families (brass, percussion, strings, woodwinds)
- Notation, instruments, dynamics all written in the score by the composer
- Piano became very popular.
- Secular music was more prevalent than sacred.

Listening Selections: *Gloria (from Heiligmesse)* by Haydn (Classical)
Gloria in Excelsis (from Gloria) by Vivaldi (Baroque)

Directions: Demonstrate your understanding of the difference between Baroque Era and Classical Era music by comparing these two pieces which have similar texts and similar composer intent. Listen to the two "Gloria" recordings. Place a check mark in the appropriate column "classical" or "baroque" beside each statement. Note that both columns may be checked, if necessary.

Characteristic	Haydn – Classical	Vivaldi – Baroque
1. Accompanied vocal music		
2. More frequent cadences (obvious phrase endings)		
3. More elaborate ornamentation (grace notes, etc.)		
4. Text based on the Catholic mass		
5. Latin text		
6. Tuneful, singable melodies		
7. Accompaniment maintains steady 8th notes throughout		
8. Accompaniment patterns change		
9. Composed for SATB chorus		

CLASSICAL ERA QUIZ

NAME ____

DATE ____

1. The Classical Era lasted from
   A. 1750-1820
   B. 1500-1600
   C. 1850-1900
2. Composers were employed to entertain
   A. wealthy nobles and aristocrats
   B. farmers and migrant workers
   C. priests and church members
3. The instrument that replaced the harpsichord was the
   A. trumpet
   B. viola
   C. piano
4. The favorite form of chamber music was the
   A. string trio
   B. string quartet
   C. string quintet
5. A work for orchestra with four contrasting parts or movements is the
   A. concerto
   B. mass
   C. symphony
6. The invention of a mechanical device that helps musicians count steadily was a
   A. time signature
   B. metronome
   C. rhythm
7. Name two composers of the Classical Era
   -
   -
8. A famous artist in the Classical Era was
   A. Goya
   B. Wordsworth
   C. Napoleon
9. Match the following books with the name of the author

_____ *Candide*	A. Samuel Johnson
_____ *Faust*	B. Jane Austen
_____ *Dictionary*	C. Voltaire
_____ *Pride and Prejudice*	D. Goethe

10. Extra credit: For what are the people in Question 8 known?

THE ROMANTIC ERA

1820 | 1840 | 1860 | 1880 | 1900

MUSIC

The last compositions of Beethoven were among the first of the new *Romantic* era, lasting from the early 1800's to about 1900. No longer employed by churches or nobles, composers became free from Classical restraints and expressed their personal emotions through their music. Instead of simple titles like *Concerto* or *Symphony*, they would often add descriptive titles like *Witches' Dance* or *To The New World*. Orchestras became larger, including nearly all the standard instruments we now use. Composers began to write much more difficult and complex music, featuring more "colorful" instrument combinations and harmonies.

Nationalism was an important trend in this era. Composers used folk music and folk legends (especially in Russia, eastern Europe and Scandinavia) to identify their music with their native lands. Today's concert audiences still generally prefer the drama of Romantic music to any other kind.

- Gioacchino Rossini *(1792–1868), William Tell Overture*
- Franz Schubert *(1797-1828), Unfinished Symphony, Tantum ergo, Die Nacht*
- Hector Berlioz *(1808-1879), Symphony fantastique, L'Enfance du Christ*
- Felix Mendelssohn *(1809-1847), In Praise of Spring, Lift Thine Eyes to the Mountains, Laudate pueri dominum*
- Robert Schumann *(1810-1856), Von dem Rosenbusch, So wahr die Sonne scheinet, In meinem Garten*
- Johannes Brahms *(1833–1897), A German Requiem, Six Folk Songs, Sleep, Gently, Sleep, Ach, arme Welt*
- Anton Bruckner *(1824-1896) Locus iste**
- Anton Dvorak *(1841–1904), If You Should Go Away*

1820 | 1840 | 1860 | 1880 | 1900

ART & LITERATURE

- Charles Dickens, author *(The Pickwick Papers, David Copperfield)*
- Lewis Carroll, author *(Alice In Wonderland)*
- Vincent van Gogh, artist *(The Sunflowers)*
- Rudyard Kipling, author *(Jungle Book)*
- Louisa May Alcott, author *(Little Women)*
- Pierre Renoir, artist *(Luncheon of the Boating Party)*
- Jules Verne, author *(20,000 Leagues Under The Sea)*
- Claude Monet, artist *(Gare Saint-Lazare)*
- Harriet Beecher Stowe, author *(Uncle Tom's Cabin)*
- Mark Twain, author *(Tom Sawyer, Huckleberry Finn)*

1820 | 1840 | 1860 | 1880 | 1900

WORLD EVENTS

- Darwin's "Origin of Species" *(1859)*
- First railroad *(1830)*
- American Civil War *(1861–1865)*
- Samuel Morse invents telegraph *(1837)*
- Emancipation Proclamation *(1863)*
- First photography *(1838)*
- Alexander Graham Bell invents telephone *(1876)*
- Slavery outlawed in England *(1833)*
- Edison invents phonograph, practical light bulb, movie projector *(1877–1888)*
- Queen Victoria is Queen of England *(1837-1901)*

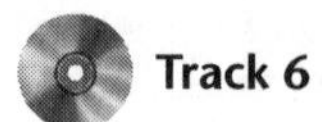
Track 6

ROMANTIC ERA 1820-1900

NAME ______________________________

DATE ______________________________

Typical Characteristics of Romantic Music
- Personal expression is the norm.
- Use of widely varying dynamic levels.
- Many expressive changes (dynamics, tempo, number of players or parts) are present in a single piece.
- There is an interest in both large forms (symphonies) and short miniature pieces.
- Solo voice and piano works (called art songs or Lieder) are very popular.
- Use of widely varying melodies (narrow range, wide range, very singable).
- Rhythmic diversity, many slight changes in tempo (rubato) is found.
- Solo piano is very popular.
- Texts indicate an interest in nature, the bizarre and the supernatural.
- Much larger orchestra is the norm.
- New instruments are added (tuba, saxophone).
- Composers specify even more details in the score (dynamic levels, tempo changes, etc.).

Listening Selection: *In Praise of Spring* by Felix Mendelssohn (1809-1847)

Directions: Listen to the recording as many times as necessary to answer the following.

1. Which voice part has the melody throughout?

   Soprano Alto Tenor Bass

2. Generally all voice parts seem to be singing the same words at the same time, especially in the middle section.

   True False

3. How many different voice parts would you guess you hear singing at once?

   1 2 3 4 5 6

4. Texture with only one voice part singing might be considered a thin texture. How would you classify the texture on *In Praise of Spring?* (circle one)

   Thick Medium Thin

5. On the back of this page list the Romantic Era characteristics which are present in *In Praise of Spring.*

ROMANTIC ERA QUIZ

NAME ____

DATE ____

1. The Romantic Era lasted from
   A. 1820-1900
   B. 1520-1600
   C. 1620-1700

2. Who wrote his first compositions in the Classical Era and his last in the Romantic Era?
   A. Mozart
   B. Haydn
   C. Beethoven

3. An important trend in this era was
   A. Imperialism
   B. Nationalism
   C. Socialism

4. Romantic music was usually very
   A. dramatic
   B. grammatic
   C. problematic

5. *Tom Sawyer* and *Huckleberry Finn* were both written by
   A. Louise May Alcott
   B. Charles Dickens
   C. Mark Twain

6. "The Sunflowers" was a painting by
   A. Vincent van Gogh
   B. Claude Monet
   C. Pierre Renoir

7. Name one thing that was invented during the Romantic Era that still exists today. Then describe how this invention has affected our lives.

THE 20th CENTURY

1900 1925 1950 1975 2000

MUSIC

The *20th century* was a diverse era of new ideas that "broke the rules" of traditional music. Styles of music moved in many different directions.

Impressionist composers Debussy and Ravel wrote music that seems more vague and blurred than the Romantics. New slightly-dissonant chords were used, and like Impressionist paintings, much of their music describes an impression of nature.

Composer Arnold Schoenberg devised a way to throw away all the old ideas of harmony by creating *12-tone* music. All 12 tones of the chromatic scale were used equally, with no single pitch forming a "key center."

Some of the music of Stravinsky and others was written in a *Neo-Classical* style (or "new" classical). This was a return to the Classical principals of balance and form, and to music that did *not* describe any scene or emotion.

Composers have experimented with many ideas: some music is based on the laws of chance, some is drawn on graph paper, some lets the performers decide when or what to play, and some is combined with electronic or other sounds.

Popular music like jazz, country, folk, and rock & roll has had a significant impact on 20th century life and has influenced great composers like Aaron Copland and Leonard Bernstein. And the new technology of computers and electronic instruments has had a major effect on the ways music is composed, performed and recorded.

- Claude Debussy *(1862–1918), Qu'il la fait bon regarder!, Beau Soir*
- J. Rosamond Johnson *(1873-1954), Lift Ev'ry Voice and Sing*
- Sergei Rachmaninoff *(1873–1943), Ave Maria*
- W.C. Handy *(1873–1958), St. Louis Blues*
- Norman Dello Joio *(1913-), Of Crows and Clusters*
- Cecil Effinger *(1914-1990), Basket from Four Pastorales*
- Vincent Persichetti *(1915-1987) sam was a man*
- Houston Bright *(1916-1970) Lament of the Enchantress, Never Tell Thy Love*
- Daniel Pinkham *(1923-)*
- Leonard Bernstein *(1918–1990), West Side Story*
- *Thea Musgrave (1928-)*
- *Pauline Oliveros (1932-)*
- *Libby Larson (1950-)*
- Augusta Read Thomas (1964-)

1900 1925 1950 1975 2000

ART & LITERATURE

- Robert Frost, author *(Stopping by Woods on a Snowy Evening)*
- Pablo Picasso, artist *(Three Musicians)*
- J.R.R. Tolkien, author *(The Lord of the Rings)*
- F. Scott Fitzgerald, author *(The Great Gatsby)*
- Andy Warhol, artist *(Pop art)*
- Salvador Dali, artist *(Soft Watches)*
- Norman Mailer, author *(The Executioner's Song)*
- John Steinbeck, author *(The Grapes of Wrath)*
- Ernest Hemingway, author *(For Whom the Bell Tolls)*
- Andrew Wyeth, artist *(Christina's World)*
- George Orwell, author *(1984)*

1900 1925 1950 1975 2000

WORLD EVENTS

- First airplane flight *(1903)*
- Television invented *(1927)*
- Berlin Wall built *(1961)*
- Destruction of Berlin Wall *(1989)*
- Titanic Sinks *(1912)*
- World War I *(1914–1918)*
- World War II *(1939–1945)*
- John F. Kennedy assassinated *(1963)*
- First radio program *(1920)*
- Civil rights march in Alabama *(1965)*
- 19th Amendment passes, Women gain right to vote *(1920)*
- First satellite launched *(1957)*
- First walk on the moon *(1969)*
- Vietnam War ends *(1975)*
- Personal computers *(1975)*

TWENTIETH CENTURY 1900-2000

NAME ____________________

DATE ____________________

Typical Characteristics of Twentieth Century Music

- Variety is the norm.
- Many composers write in styles that had not existed before.
- Many composers continue to write in all previous styles.
- Composers revert back to ancient styles and combine them with newer styles.
- Composers combine popular styles with serious styles (jazz with symphonic works for example).
- Much rhythmic variety is popular.
- Mixed meter (changing from triple to duple in all combinations) becomes common.
- Rhythmic emphasis (jazz and world music influences) is prevalent.
- Dissonant harmonies become more typical.
- Instead of using consonant thirds (combining C and E or F and A for example), dissonant chords are common (chords containing notes half steps or whole steps apart).
- Aleatoric music (sections performed by chance) begins. For example, each singer repeats a phrase over and over, but enters whenever and at whatever tempo he or she sees fit. Thus each performance is always different.
- Spoken as well as sung words are used for specific effects.
- A cappella singing continues; but choirs with piano remain the norm.
- Accompaniments vary widely with much use of different accompanying instruments.

Listening Selections: *Praise the Name of God with a Song* by Allen Koepke
Glorificamus te by Eugene Butler

Directions: Listen to the recordings as many times as necessary to determine the characteristics of each song. Check the appropriate boxes below.

Characteristic	*Praise the Name*	*Glorificamus te*
1. Uses dissonant harmonies		
2. Uses mixed meters		
3. Uses a reference to Gregorian chant		
4. Uses male and female voices		
5. Uses female voices		
6. Includes aleatoric passages		
7. Includes highly rhythmic passages		
8. Uses piano acompaniment		
9. Uses an ancient text		

- Would you mistake either recording as coming from a different time period? Why or why not?

TWENTIETH CENTURY QUIZ

NAME ________________________________

DATE ________________________________

1. Twentieth Century music was written during the
   A. 1900s
   B. 1600s
   C. 1800s

2. Impressionistic music was written by
   A. Ravel and Debussy
   B. Bach and Beethoven
   C. Schoenberg and Stravinsky

3. Neo-classical music returned to the principles of balance and form that prevailed during the
   A. Baroque Era
   B. Romantic Era
   C. Classical Era

4. Twelve-tone music was written so that it used
   A. 12 different key signatures
   B. 12 different tones of the chromatic scale
   C. 12 different rhythms

5. The way music was composed, performed and recorded was greatly influenced by
   A. technique
   B. technicality
   C. technology

6. Match the following books with the name of the author.

_____ *The Great Gatsby*	A. Ernest Hemingway
_____ *The Grapes of Wrath*	B. F. Scott Fitzgerald
_____ *For Whom the Bell Tolls*	C. John Steinbach

7. Name two famous visual artists of the Twentieth Century.
   •
   •

8. Name three world events that occurred during the Twentieth Century.
   •
   •
   •

9. Select one event from Question 8 and write a paragraph on how it has influenced life today.

LISTENING LESSONS

- **General Listening**
- **Listening for Form**
- **Listening for Balance**
- **Spirituals Old and New**
- **Global Folk Songs**

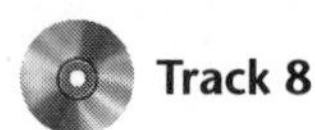
Track 8

LISTENING

POLYPHONIC ENTRANCES

NAME ____________________

DATE ____________________

Listening Selection: *Psallite* **by Michael Praetorius (1571-1621)**

About the Composer:
Michael Praetorius (1571-1621) was a German music theorist and composer who began his musical career as an organist in 1604. He spent much of his later years writing a musical encyclopedia which was a comprehensive look at the music and style of his age. Praetorius is considered a composer from the early Baroque period of music history.

About the Times:
- Galileo identifies gravity (1602)
- First English colony in America (Jamestown, 1607)
- First African slave to America (1619)

New Vocabulary:
When different voice parts enter at different times, that music is called **polyphonic**. Polyphonic means "many sounds." In a song in which all singers enter together singing the identical music, it is known as **monophonic** (one sound) or unison. When singers enter together but sing different notes (sing in harmony), it is known as **homophonic** (same sound).

Listening Activity:
Listen to the opening measures of *Psallite* several times, then answer the questions.

1. Do the voice parts enter together or at different times?
   Together   Different Times

2. Number the voice parts in the order in which they enter
   _____ Soprano (highest women's voice)
   _____ Alto (lowest women's voice)
   _____ Tenor (highest men's voice)
   _____ Bass (lowest men's voice)

3. Would you consider the opening section of *Psallite* to be polyphonic, monophonic, or homophonic?

4. Music may be expressive even if the text is in an unfamiliar language. Which word or words would best describe the mood expressed in *Psallite?*
   peaceful   active   solemn   joyful   depressing
   puzzling   fun

5. Describe how a song might sound today if a modern composer created a piece in the same mood.

UNISON • HARMONY

NAME ____

DATE ____

Listening Selection: ***Make a Song for My Heart to Sing*** **by Julie Knowles**

New Vocabulary:
Groups of voices may sing the same pitches (singing in unison) and groups of voices may also sing two different pitches at the same time (singing in harmony). Careful listening is necessary to hear the difference between unison and harmony.

Listening Activity:
Listen carefully to *Make a Song for My Heart to Sing*. After each section, circle "Unison" or "Harmony" depending on what you hear.

What can I do at the end of the day to show my thanks in my own special way?
I'll take all my happiness and love that it brings and make a song for my heart to sing.

1. Unison or Harmony

I'll sing it high, sing it low, sing it every where I go
Then far and wide, it's a feeling from inside.

2. Unison or Harmony

How do you feel when the day is at end?
Did you take time to be somebody's friend?
Think of the good times a new friend can bring
and make a song for your heart to sing.

3. Unison or Harmony

Then sing it high, sing it low, sing it every where you go.
Then far and wide, can't you feel it from inside.

4. Unison or Harmony

What can I do at the end of the day, To show my thanks in my own special way?
I'll take all my happiness and love that it brings and make a song for my heart to sing.

5. Unison or Harmony

Listening Extension:
Explain the harmony-unison pattern that composer Julie Knowles used. Did you notice any pattern that the composer established? Did she always harmonize certain sections? Did she always put the same sections in unison?

**Reminder: Always be aware whether you are singing in unison or harmony.
It will make you a much better choral singer.**

WHO HAS THE MELODY?

NAME ______________________________

DATE ______________________________

Listening Selection: *Cripple Creek* by Emily Crocker

Listening Activity:
When two parts are singing together in harmony, can you hear which part has the melody and which part has the harmony? The melody in *Cripple Creek* switches frequently between Part I (the higher part) and Part II (the lower part). Listen carefully to *Cripple Creek* to see if your ears can identify which part has the melody. Write a check mark in column "Part I" when Part I sings the melody and write a check mark in column "Part II" when Part II sings the melody. You may need to listen several times.

WHO HAS THE MELODY?	PART I	PART II
1. Johnny's got a gal at the head of the creek		
2. Goes up to see her about the middle of the week.		
3. Just like an apple from the tree		
4. Sweetest little gal you ever did see.		
5. Goin' up Cripple Creek,		
6. Goin' in a run		
7. Goin' up Cripple Creek		
8. Have a little fun.		
9. Goin' up Cripple Creek		
10. Goin' in a whirl,		
11. Goin' up Cripple Creek to see his girl.	UNISON SINGING	
12. Cripple Creek's wide and Cripple Creek's deep		
13. He'll wade Cripple Creek before he sleeps.		
14. Rolls up his britches to his knees,		
15. He'll wade Cripple Creek whenever he please.		
16. Goin' up Cripple Creek, Goin' in a run,	BOTH PARTS EQUAL	
17. Goin' up Cripple Creek to have a little fun.	BOTH PARTS EQUAL	
18. Goin' up Cripple Creek, Goin' in a whirl,	BOTH PARTS EQUAL	
19. Goin' up Cripple Creek to see his girl.	BOTH PARTS EQUAL	
20. Halfway there he stops to rest		
21. Thinks about the gal that he loves best.		
22. Picks him a watermelon fresh off the vine,		
23. Spittin' them seeds sure do feel fine!		
24. Goin' up Cripple Creek, Goin' in a run,	BOTH PARTS EQUAL	
25. Goin' up Cripple Creek to have a little fun.	BOTH PARTS EQUAL	
26. Goin' up Cripple Creek, Goin' in a whirl,	BOTH PARTS EQUAL	
27. Goin' up Cripple Creek to see his girl.	BOTH PARTS EQUAL	
(repeat Numbers 24-27)		

Reminder: Singing in harmony is great fun, but balance is important. The melody part should be a bit louder than the harmony part. It is important to know which part you are singing at all times.

DYNAMIC CONTRASTS

NAME ____________________

DATE ____________________

Listening Selection: ***Charlotte-Town*** **by Emily Crocker**

New Vocabulary:

Dynamic contrasts (changes in loud and soft in music) are one of the most important ways to make music interesting and expressive. The dynamic terms we use are Italian terms and are abbreviated as shown below.

forte (*f*) = loud   piano (*p*) = soft

Listening Activity:

As you listen to *Charlotte-Town*, fill in each blank with the appropriate dynamic abbreviation, *f* for loud and *p* for soft. You may need to listen several times.

Hey Ho! The boatmen row! Floatin' down the river on the Ohio!
Hey Ho! The boatmen row! Floatin' down the river on the Ohio! (1)__________

Charlotte-town's burnin' down, Hey Ho! The boatmen row!
Burnin' down to the ground. Good bye Liza Jane.
Ain't-cha mighty sorry, (2)__________
Good-bye, good-bye. (3)__________
Ain't-cha mighty sorry! (4)__________
Good-bye Liza Jane! (5)__________

Black my boots and a make them shine. Hey Ho! The boatmen row!
Black my boots and a make them shine. Good-bye Liza Jane.
Ain't-cha mighty sorry, (6)__________
Good-bye, good-bye. (7)__________
Ain't-cha mighty sorry! (8)__________
Good-bye Liza Jane! (9)__________

There's a gal in Baltimore, good-bye, good-bye.
Silver doorplate on her door, Good-bye Liza Jane!
Ain't-cha mighty sorry, (10)__________
Good-bye, good-bye. (11)__________
Ain't-cha mighty sorry! (12)__________
Good-bye Liza-Jane. (13)__________

Listening Extension:

There are more dynamic terms available to singers, to show even greater distinction between loud and soft. Listen again to Charlotte-Town and see if one of the following terms could be substituted for what you wrote.

fortissimo (*ff*) = very loud   pianissimo (*pp*) = very soft
mezzo forte (*mf*) = medium loud   mezzo piano (*mp*) = medium soft

LISTENING FOR FORM: STROPHIC

NAME ____________________

DATE ____________________

Listening Selection: ***Cripple Creek*** **by Emily Crocker**

Listening Activity:
Label the first section "A." Label the second section "B", because the music of the second section is different from the music of the first section. Continue on, labeling each box as "A" or "B" depending on if it is the same or different from "A."

1. _A_ *Johnny's got a gal at the head of the creek. Goes up to see her 'bout the middle of the week . . .*
2. _B_ *Goin' up Cripple Creek, Goin' in a run. Goin' up Cripple Creek Have a little fun. Goin' up Cripple Creek . . .*
3. ____ *Cripple Creek's wide and Cripple Creek's deep. He'll wade Cripple Creek before he sleeps . . .*
4. ____ *Goin' up Cripple Creek, Goin' in a run, Goin' up Cripple Creek to have a little fun. Goin' up Cripple Creek . . .*
5. ____ *Halfway there he stops to rest. Thinks about the gal that he loves best . . .*
6. ____ *Goin' up Cripple Creek, Goin' in a run, Goin' up Cripple Creek to have a little fun. Goin' up Cripple Creek . . .*
7. ____ *Goin' up Cripple Creek, Goin' in a run, Goin' up Cripple Creek to have a little fun. Goin' up Cripple Creek . . .*
8. ____ *Goin' up Cripple Creek to see his girl!* (NOTE: special ending section is called a Coda.)
9. Look at the pattern of your A and B answers. Circle the pattern which best fits.
   ABABABB Coda ABBABBA Coda ABAAABA Coda
10. Which sections have the same <u>melody</u> and the same <u>words</u>? (circle one)
    A sections B sections
11. When one section repeats the same music <u>and</u> the same words, the form is called Verse and Chorus. Verse sections repeat melodies, but change words. Chorus sections repeat melodies and words. (circle your answer)
    - **A** Is *Cripple Creek* an example of Verse and Chorus? Yes No
    - **B** Which part is *Goin' up Cripple Creek, Goin' in a run. . .?* Verse Chorus
12. A Verse and Chorus song is also referred to as **strophic** song.
    - **A** Is *Cripple Creek* written in strophic form? Yes No
    - **B** Write a definition of strophic form.

LISTENING FOR FORM: ABA

NAME ____________________

DATE ____________________

Listening Selection: ***Psallite*** **by Michael Praetorius (1571-1621)**

New Vocabulary:
ABA form is one of the most common forms (structure of repeating sections) in music. In this structure a section of music (A) is performed, a contrasting, different section is performed next (B), and the beginning section (A) is repeated.
ABA = Same • Different • Same.

Background Information:
Psallite has three sections. The first section begins in Latin:
"Psallite, unigenito, Christo Dei Filio . . .

The second section begins in German:
"Ein kleines Kindelein liegt in dem Krippelein . . .

The third section begins again in Latin:
"Psallite unigenito . . ."

Note: It may be difficult to tell where the second section ends and the third section begins. Listen closely to hear the amazing compositional thing that Praetorius did when connecting the second and third sections.

Listening Activity:
Listen to *Psallite.* Answer the following questions to help guide your search for what Praetorius did to connect the second and third sections.

1. Can you clearly hear the ending of the first section? Yes No
2. What makes it easy to hear the ending of the first section?
3. Is the second section the same or different from the first section?
4. Can you clearly hear the ending of the second section? Yes No
5. What clues did you use to figure out when the second section ended? Possible answers might be: "The ending section begins to sound like the first section so second section must be over." or "I started listening for a third section after the second section had played as long as the first section." Your reason:
6. What unusual thing did Praetorius do to connect the second and third sections?
7. Based on what you have learned, is *Psallite* in ABA form? Yes No

LISTENING FOR FORM: REPETITION OF SECTIONS

NAME ____________________

DATE ____________________

Listening Selection: ***Ju Me Leve un Bel Maitín*** **(In the Morning I Arose)**
15th Century Villancico edited by Robert L. Goodale

More About Form:
Both ABA and Strophic (Verse • Chorus) forms are very popular and are much used from earliest times to the modern day. Some forms have repeating sections, but do not really follow the strophic pattern. *Ju Me Leve un Bel Maitín* is an example of such a piece. To analyze the form, use the familiar A and B. For additional different sections you may even need a C or D.

Background Information:
Ju Me Leve un Bel Maitín is a 15th Century Villancico which is a "type of Spanish poetry, idyllic or amorous in subject matter" and usually sung as a lively dance. This particular villancico tells the story of a person speaking to a nightingale. The final lines translate as "Nightingale, fly away with this message. Tell my lover this for me: I am already married." *Ju Me Leve un Bel Maitín* combines three languages – Spanish, French, and Catalan. The repeated words, *"Din di rin din"* are nonsense syllables.

Listening Activity:
Based on listening to this piece, answer the following questions.

1. How can you tell where one section ends and another one begins in *Ju Me Leve un Bel Maitín?*

2. Using letters, label the sections of *Ju Me Leve un Bel Maitín.*

Section 1. ____________	Section 5. ____________
Section 2. ____________	Section 6. ____________
Section 3. ____________	Section 7. ____________
Section 4. ____________	

3. Circle the pattern of sections which you found.

ABAAAAA ABCCCAA ABCDCAA

LISTENING FOR BALANCE

NAME ______________________________

DATE ______________________________

Listening selection: ***O occhi manza mia*** **(Thine Eyes, O My Beloved)**
by Orlando di Lasso (1532-1594)

New Vocabulary:
Balance refers to the loudness or softness of individual sections as compared to the other sections of the choir. This listening activity is designed to call your attention to issues of balance.

Listening Activity:

1. Circle Your Voice Part: Soprano Alto Tenor Bass

2. Listen to the first phrase of *O occhi manza mia.* (about 15 seconds)

3. Check the voice part to which you paid the most attention:
   _____ I heard mostly the soprano part
   _____ I heard mostly the alto part
   _____ I heard mostly the tenor part
   _____ I heard mostly the bass part
   _____ I heard all four parts equally

4. Now listen to the next four examples in which one voice part has been deliberately mixed so that it sounds stronger than the other three. Evaluate the balance on these performances.
   a. Soprano part stronger
      _____ This sounded about right to me
      _____ This sounded wrong to me
   b. Alto part stronger
      _____ This sounded about right to me
      _____ This sounded wrong to me
   c. Tenor part stronger:
      _____ This sounded about right to me
      _____ This sounded wrong to me
   d. Bass part stronger
      _____ This sounded about right to me
      _____ This sounded wrong to me

5. Compare your answers with others in your class.
   a. Number of people agreeing with you. ________
   b. Number of people disagreeing with you. _________
   c. Number of people who sing your voice part who agreed with you. ______

6. Why do you think there was not 100% agreement in what people heard?

SPIRITUALS OLD AND NEW

NAME ______________________________

DATE ______________________________

Listening Selection: ***Steal Away,*** **traditional spiritual arranged by Marshall Bartholomew**
Elijah Rock, **traditional spiritual arranged by Moses Hogan**

About African-American Spirituals:
The spiritual may include simple unison melodies as well as thicker textures with a strong emphasis on rhythm. The traditional melodies, originally conceived by African slaves in the years prior to the American Civil War, were declarations of faith ranging from haunting melodies to fast tunes with rhythmic dance-like character. Over the years, spirituals have been arranged for choirs into powerful concert pieces.

These two arrangements are very different in many ways, yet they both reveal the heritage of the spiritual. Marshall Bartholomew arranged the familiar *Steal Away* for the Yale Glee Club sometime prior to 1953. Moses Hogan arranged the familiar *Elijah Rock* in 1994. In this worksheet, you will compare and contrast the two spirituals.

Listening Activity:

1. First Impressions
   Listen to the first 40 seconds of *Steal Away,* then immediately listen to the first 40 seconds of *Elijah Rock.* List your first impressions regarding the obvious differences between the two.

   ____
   ____
   ____

2. Considered Reflection
   Listen to complete performances of both Steal Away and *Elijah Rock.* Consider the musical and expressive similarities between the two pieces.

   ____
   ____
   ____

3. Composer Intent
   How would the composer intend for his audience to feel at the end of the piece? Consider whether it is possible for two different pieces to have similar musical intentions.

   ____
   ____
   ____

4. Advanced Considerations
   Thick textures. Both pieces may be said to have thick textures. What musical factors contribute to a sense of texture in these pieces? Can your ear separate rhythmic complexity from harmonic complexity?

Track 17, 18 & 19

LISTENING

GLOBAL FOLK SONGS

NAME ____________________

DATE ____________________

Listening Selections:

¿Que Regalo? from *Three Spanish Carols* arranged by Emily Crocker (Spanish)
Sansa Kroma arranged by Emily Crocker (African)
S'vivon arranged by Gregg Smith (Hebrew)

Background Information:

¿Que Regalo? is a well-known Spanish Christmas carol, and is translated as "What shall I bring to the Child in the manger?"

Sansa Kroma is an African playground song from Ghana. It tells the reassuring story of how young animals are often orphaned and must survive on their own, but children need not worry, for if orphaned they will be taken in and cared for by relatives and friends.

S'vivon is a Jewish game played during Hanukkah using a four-sided top (dreydl). Each side of a dreydl has a Hebrew initial of the phrase "Great Miracle Happened There." All ages spin the dreydl. Presents are given out based on which Hebrew letter is showing when the dreydl stops.

Listening Activity:

1. Select the two songs which are the most similar and explain your reasons. Did you focus on text? On music? On style? On tempo? Other?

2. Select the two songs which are the most different and explain your reasons.

3. Which one is your favorite? Why? What do you especially like about it?

4. In your opinion, what factors might connect all of these songs in any way even though they are geographically very different?

5. Look through your choral text and see how many other global folk songs you can find. List them below.

MUSIC ACROSS THE CURRICULUM

- **Music and Reading**
- **Music and Writing**
- **Music and Social Studies**
- **Music and Math**

 Track 20

READING COMPREHENSION

NAME ______________________________

DATE ______________________________

Music Selection: ***Shenandoah,*** **American folk song arranged by Linda Spevacek**

Background Information:
The story behind *Shenandoah* is said to have many origins. Some sources say that the song was about a fur trader wooing the daughter of an Indian chief. One version speaks of a sailor who courts a girl named Sally for "seven long years" but is rejected because he is a "dirty sailor." Sometimes the word Shenandoah refers to a river in Virginia, or to a region (the Shenandoah River valley) or to the people who live in that region. Regardless, this beautiful tune and the word Shenandoah appear over and over in American history, usually with slightly different texts and slight variations in melody, but are always recognizable as the same song.

Directions: Carefully read the text while listening to this beautiful song, then answer the questions.

0 Shenandoah, I long to see you. Away you rollin' river.
0 Shenandoah, I long to see you.
Away, we're bound away, cross the wide Missouri.

0 Shenandoah, I long to hear you, Away you rollin' river.
0 Shenandoah, I long to hear you.
Away, we're bound away, cross the wide Missouri.

1. How could a song take on so many different meanings?

2. Why would people want to use the same tune over and over?

3. What can you infer about the meaning of the text in this arrangement of *Shenandoah?*

READING COMPREHENSION

NAME ____________________

DATE ____________________

Music Selection: ***Sound the Trumpet*** **by Henry Purcell**

Background Information:
Sound the Trumpet was written in 1694 by the English composer, Henry Purcell. "Hautboy" (pronounced oh-Boy) was an early instrument similar to the oboe of today.

Directions: Carefully read the text of this song without listening to the recording of the work, then answer Question 1. After listening to a recording of *Sound the Trumpet,* answer the rest of the questions.

Sound the trumpet, sound the trumpet. Sound. Sound.
Till around you make the listening shores rebound,
Make the listening shores rebound.

On the sprightly hautboy, On the sprightly hautboy,
Play all the instruments of joy that skillful numbers can employ
To celebrate, to celebrate
The glories of this day.

1. What is the mood of this text? List specific words from the text that led to your conclusion.

   A Mood:

   B Specific words:

2. Now listen to a recording of *Sound the Trumpet.* Does the music contribute to or detract from the overall mood of the text? State reasons for your answer.

3. Decide whether this piece was written for a religious or a non-religious occasion. Identify ideas from the text and the music recording which support your reasoning.

READING COMPREHENSION

NAME ____

DATE ____

Music Selection: *Turtle Dove,* **arranged by Linda Spevacek**

Directions: Study the text of this beautiful song, then answer the questions.

Fare you well, my dear, I must be gone and leave you for awhile.
If I roam away, I'll come back again
Tho I roam ten thousand miles, my dear . . .

So fair thou art, my bonny lad (lass), so deep in love am I
But I never will prove false to the bonny lad (lass) I love,
Till the starts fall from the sky, my dear . . .

The sea will never run dry, my dear,
Nor the rocks ever melt with the sun.
But I never will prove false to the bonny lad (lass) I love,
Till the stars fall from the sky, till the stars fall from the sky.

0 yonder sits that little turtle dove. He doth sit on yonder high tree.
A making a moan for the loss of his love.
As I will do for thee, my dear, As I will do for thee.
Fare you well my dear, fare you well, farewell, farewell.

1. Define the meaning of "fare" and "fair" as they are used in this song.

2. In your opinion, how many people are speaking in this song? Why?

3. Listen to a recording of this song. Does hearing the recording change any of your answers or your thoughts about *Turtle Dove?* If so, please explain.

4. What do you think ultimately happened to the people in this song?

READING COMPREHENSION

NAME ______________________________

DATE ______________________________

Title of Song: ______________________________

1. Carefully read the text of the assigned song. What is the song about? In your own words, summarize the meaning of this text. Be sure to use correct grammar, spelling and punctuation.

2. Describe the mood or emotion of this song.

3. After listening to or learning to sing this song, how do you feel the music contributes to the meaning of the words?

4. How will you sing the song differently now that you have analyzed the meaning of the text?

 Track 10

READING COMPREHENSION

NAME ______________________________

DATE ______________________________

Music Selection: ***Cripple Creek*** **by Emily Crocker**

Directions: Read the words to Cripple Creek as you listen to the recording, then answer the questions.

Johnny's got a gal at the head of the creek. Goes up to see her 'bout the middle of the week. Just like an apple from the tree, Sweetest little gal you ever did see.

Refrain
Goin' up Cripple Creek, Goin' in a run. Goin' up Cripple Creek have a little fun.
Goin' up Cripple Creek , Goin' in a whirl, Goin' up Cripple Creek to see his girl.

Cripple Creek's wide and Cripple Creek's deep. He'll wade Cripple Creek before he sleeps. Rolls up his britches to his knees, He'll wade Cripple Creek whenever he please.
Refrain

Halfway there he stops to rest. Thinks about the gal that he loves best.
Picks him a watermelon fresh off the vine, Spittin' them seeds sure do feel fine!
Refrain

1. Assume that Cripple Creek is a real place. Answer these questions to the best of your ability.
   a. Cripple Creek might be in what part of the country?

   b. Cripple Creek might be in which state?

   c. Johnny and his girl might be how old?

   d. Why is Johnny crossing Cripple Creek?

   e. List specific words from the text which lead you to believe that Johnny is anxious to see his girl.

2. Assume that Cripple Creek does not refer to a real place. What might Cripple Creek represent besides a wide creek? Discuss your answer.

READING COMPREHENSION

NAME ______________________________

DATE ______________________________

Title of Song: ______________________________

Directions: Read the text carefully. Jot down some key words of the text to help you determine the meaning of the text. List any words of which you do not know the meaning. Either through class discussion or use of a dictionary, write the meaning of the unfamiliar words.

What is the song about? Using your own words, summarize the meaning of this text. Be sure to use correct grammar, spelling and punctuation. Please write in complete sentences.

 Track 12

WRITING - PART 1

NAME ______________________________

DATE ______________________________

Music Selection: ***Ju Me Leve un Bel Maitín*** **edited by Goodale**

Directions: Listen to the recording of *Ju Me Leve un Bel Maitín.* Although this song is not in English, discuss in writing what this song might be about. (Hints: Is it sacred or secular? Joyful or sorrowful? Moody or uplifting? Serious or playful?) Write in complete sentences to explain your thoughts.

WRITING - PART 2

NAME ______________________________

DATE ______________________________

Music Selection: ***Ju Me Leve un Bel Maitín*** **edited by Goodale**

Directions: Complete Writing – Part 1 in which you discussed the meaning of the music without looking at an English translation. Now listen to *Ju Me Leve Un Bel Maitín* and read an English translation of the text.

Early in the morning I rose and walked through the meadow.
I met a nightingale who was singing high in the trees.
I said to him, "0 nightingale, fly away and take this message. . .
Please tell my lover for me that I am already married!"

Note: *Dindirindin* is a series of nonsense syllables.

Consider the meaning of the words. Write an essay comparing your answer before and after reading the English translation. What effect does the music have on your understanding of the meaning of a text?

WRITING

NAME ____________________

DATE ____________________

Robert Shaw (1916 – 1999), the renowned choral conductor, has stated that virtually all choral errors are errors in rhythmic precision. Consider what he meant and then write an essay supporting or arguing against his theory. Use musical ideas to support your position.

WRITING

NAME ____

DATE ____

Directions: Answer the following questions in essay form using one paragraph per question. Please write with complete sentences and be prepared to discuss your ideas in class.

Concert Title ______________________________ Concert Date______________

1. Musically speaking, what was the strongest song or portion of the program. Why?

2. Musically speaking, what was the weakest portion of the program. Why?

3. Musically speaking, what did you enjoy most about the concert?

4. Share comments your parents, friends or teachers made about the concert.

WRITING

NAME ____________________

DATE ____________________

Directions: The Melody School District school board has just voted to eliminate all Fine Arts activities from the school curriculum. You have been selected to serve on a committee to make a presentation to the Melody school board on the importance of music classes in the schools. Include in your presentation reasons choir class is important to the entire development of the student. Include three or more of the following aspects: developing social skills, working as a team, cooperation, commitment, practice, high level thinking skills, emotional expression, public performances, competition, music appreciation, career preparation or other ideas. Be persuasive in your thoughts.

Organize your essay to include an introduction, a body, and a conclusion.

WRITING

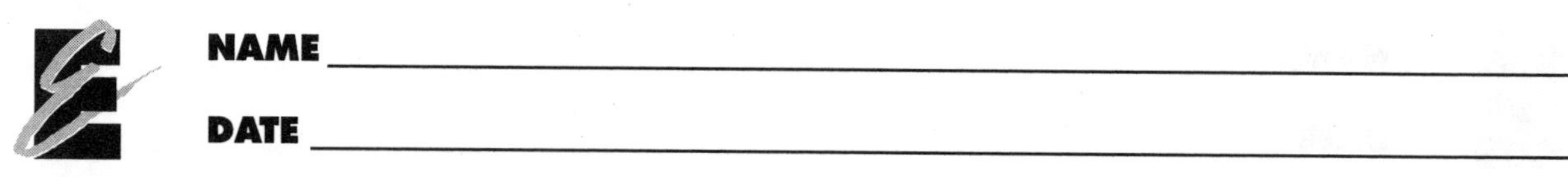

Directions: You have been selected to introduce the program at the next elementary school tour (grades 3-5). Write an introduction to three songs we are currently singing, using words that would be of interest to a younger audience. Give them enough information about the music to enjoy the concert.

Song Title and Introduction:

Song Title and Introduction:

Song Title and Introduction:

HISTORY AND READING

NAME ______________________________

DATE ______________________________

Music Selections: ***Sound the Trumpet*** **by Henry Purcell**
In Praise of Spring **by Felix Mendelssohn**

Background Information:
These two pieces were written over a hundred years apart. Henry Purcell (1659-1695) from England was composing during the last quarter of the seventeenth century. Felix Mendelssohn (1809-1847) from Germany was composing during the early to middle nineteenth century. Listen carefully to the two recordings and answer the following:

Directions:

1. List important world/historical events that happened during the time of each composer's life. You may use your own knowledge, the timeline in the *Essential Elements for Choir Teacher Resource Kit*, or outside research for your information.

Important Events:

Henry Purcell (1659-1695)	Felix Mendelssohn (1809-1847)
1.	1.
2.	2.
3.	3.
4.	4.
5.	5.

2. Despite differences in time and culture, you will probably notice similarities between the two pieces. Based on your listening, list as many similarities as you can. Start with the similarities between the basic intent of the composer: both pieces are celebratory in nature.

   A

   B

   C

3. Consider music of today. Discuss how quickly musical styles have changed during your lifetime. Relate this to the amount of change noticeable between the Purcell and Mendelssohn examples.

AFRICAN-AMERICAN COMPOSERS

NAME ______________________________

DATE ______________________________

The works of three famous African-American composers are featured in this lesson. They are: Moses Hogan (born March 13, 1953) who arranged *Elijah Rock*, Rosamond Johnson (1873-1954) who wrote *Lift Ev'ry Voice and Sing* and W.C. Handy (1873-1958) who wrote St. Louis Blues. These are but a few of the many African-Americans who have made significant contributions to the world of music.

1. Without doing any further research, list as many African-American composers and performers you can name – living or deceased.

2. What does your list have to say about present day opportunities for African-American composers and performers?

3. What does your list have to say about the influence of African-Americans on the world of music?

4. To learn more about other African American composers, use your library, internet, and/or recordings to research information about the following composers. Share your findings with the class.

Harry T. Burleigh (1866-1949)
Scott Joplin (1868-1917)
Will Marion Cook (1869-1944)
Rosamond Johnson (1873-1954)
W.C. Handy (1873-1958)
Jelly Roll Morton (1885-1941)
William Grant Still (1895-1978)
Duke Ellington (1899-1974)
Moses Hogan (born March 13, 1953)

WOMEN COMPOSERS

NAME ______________________________

DATE ______________________________

Directions: Study the Timelines from the Twentieth Century and the Romantic Era to answer the following questions.

1. How many women composers are listed on the Twentieth Century Timeline?

2. How many women composers are listed on the Romantic Era Timeline?

3. Discuss why you think there is such a difference between the number of women listed on the Twentieth Century Timeline versus those listed on the Romantic Era Timeline.

4. What does this information have to say about present day opportunities for women composers?

5. Extension Activity.
   Research women composers from other time periods. Use your library and/or the internet. You might start by researching information about the following composers:

   Hildegard von Bingen (1098-1179)
   Francesca Caccini (l587-ca. 1640)
   Elizabeth-Claude Jacquet de la Guerre (1666-1729)
   Anna Amalia, Princess of Prussia (1723-1787)
   Clara Wieck Schumann(1819-1910)
   Amy Marcy Cheney Beach (1867-1944)
   Ellen Taaffe Zwilich (1939-)

HISPANIC COMPOSERS

NAME ______________________________

DATE ______________________________

1. Without doing any further research, list as many Hispanic composers and performers you can name – living or deceased.

2. What does your list have to say about present day opportunities for Hispanic composers and performers?

3. What does your list have to say about the influence of Hispanics on the world of music?

4. To learn more about other Hispanic composers, use your library, internet, and/or recordings to research information about the following composers. Share your findings with the class.

Cuba: Ignacio Cervantes (1847-1905)
Spain: Pablo Casals (1876-1973)
Mexico: Manuel Ponce (1882-1948)
Mexico: Silvestre Reveultas (1899-1940)
Mexico: Carlos Chavez (1899-1978)
Mexico: Luis Sandi (1905-)
Argentina: Alberto Ginastera (1916-1983)
Puerto Rico: Hector Campos-Parsi (1922-)
Argentina: Roberto Caamano (1923 -)
Argentina: Pompeyo Camps (1924 -)
Argentina: Sergio Calligaris (1941-)
Cuba: Tania Leon (1943-)

GLOBAL FOLK SONGS

NAME ______________________________

DATE ______________________________

Music Selections:
- *Elijah Rock* arranged by Moses Hogan (African-American Spiritual)
- *Ju Me Leve un Bel Maitín* arranged by Robert Goodale (Spanish, French, and Catalan)
- *¿Que Regalo?* from *Three Spanish Carols* arranged by Emily Crocker (Spanish)
- *Sansa Kroma* arranged by Emily Crocker (African)
- *S'vivon* arranged by Gregg Smith (Hebrew)

Background Information:
Elijah Rock is an African-American spiritual, one of the first truly American forms of music. Spirituals were originally developed by African slaves who longed for freedom and created songs of hope.

Ju Me Leve Un Bel Maitín comes from 15th century Spain. The text is in Spanish, French and Catalan and means "Nightingale, fly away and take this message. Tell my lover this for me: That I am already married."

¿Que Regalo? is a well-known Spanish Christmas carol, and is translated as "What shall I bring to the Child in the manger?"

Sansa Kroma is an African playground song. It tells the reassuring story of how young animals are often orphaned and must survive on their own, but children need not worry, for if orphaned they will be taken in and cared for by relatives and friends.

S'vivon is a Jewish game played during Hanukkah using a four-sided top (dreydl). Each side of a dreydl has a Hebrew initial of the phrase "Great Miracle Happened There." All ages spin the dreydl. Presents are given out based on which Hebrew letter is showing when the dreydl stops.

Directions:
1. Listen to each song from across the globe and select one of them to explore in greater depth. Use the library and/or the internet to find additional information about your chosen culture, country and/or time period.

2. Share your information with others in your class.

3. In the space below, share what you have learned about how the music you selected is unique to the culture, customs, time or region it represents.

MATHEMATICS

BAR GRAPHS

NAME ______________________________

DATE ______________________________

Directions: The number of singers on each voice part in relationship to the total number of singers in your choir plays an important role in achieving proper balance. As these numbers change, adjustments often have to be made. Use this bar graph as an aid in predicting what adjustments might have to be made to achieve proper balance in your choir.

1. Count the total number of singers in your choir. ________

2. Determine the total number of singers on each voice part:

	Voice Part	Number of singers
A	________	________
B	________	________
C	________	________
D	________	________

3. Using the information gathered above, create a bar graph representing the total number of singers in your choir and the number of singers on each voice part.

65
60
55
50
45
40
35
30
25
20
15
10
5
0

Total____ Part A____ Part B____ Part C____ Part D____

ANALYZING A BAR GRAPH

NAME ______________________________

DATE ______________________________

Directions: In the previous assignment you determined information about the number of singers in your choir. Using the information from Bar Graph Activity Sheet (p. 134), please answer the following questions:

1. Total number of singers in the choir. ______________________________

2. Total number of singers on your voice part. ______________________________

3. Your voice part makes up what percentage of the total choir? ______________
   (Number of singers on your voice part divided by the total number of singers)

4. Are the voice parts in your choir evenly distributed (approximately the same number of singers on each part)? Circle one response.

   exactly the same   fairly the same   not the same at all

5. Write a definition of the term "balance" as it applies to choral music.

6. How does the number of singers on your voice part compared to the rest of the choir affect the balance of the choir?

7. What things can you do as a singer to overcome balance problems in your choir?

PROBLEM SOLVING

NAME ______________________________

DATE ______________________________

Problem: The choir is considering producing a commemorative compact disk for the annual Homecoming festivities as a money making project. These CDs will be sold for $15.00 each. You have been asked to determine the number of CDs that must be sold to cover all costs, and the number of CDs that must be sold to make a 25% profit.

Number of CDs for first run	1,000

Cost analysis:

Cost to record, edit master tape of the performance	$3,000.00
Licensing fee for recordings	$500.00
Cost to design and print labels, in-lays and cover	$750.00
Price per CD for duplication and packaging	$.85

1. ______________ Figure the total cost to produce the first 1,000 CDs. (Add all costs including 1000 x .85)

2. ______________ How many CDs must be sold to break even? (Total cost divided by the selling price of one CD)

3. ______________ How many CDs must be sold to make a 25% profit? (25% of total cost + total cost divided by selling price of one CD)

4. ______________ For the first 1000 CDs, what is the cost per CD? (Total cost divided by 1000)

5. Analyze the information. Based on the size of your current choral program and the average annual attendance at Homecoming festivities, do you feel your choir will be able to sell the number of CDs required to make a profit? Please support your answer either way.

6. For a comparison study, do this entire exercise again with number of CDs for first run at 2,000. Then again with first run at 500. Fill in the chart below. Discuss your findings.

First Run of CDs	1000	2000	500
1. Total Cost			
2. # of CDs breakeven			
3. # of CDs 25% profit			
4. Unit cost per CD			

TEACHER GUIDE

HINTS ON GIVING GRADES IN CHOIR

Excerpted from "The Grading Game" by Dr. Janice Killian. Used with permission.

These are personal comments and opinions of the author.

Select an objective to teach, teach it, and then grade progress based on that objective. Grade your students based on what they do every day. For example, if you have chosen to emphasize expressive phrasing, then evaluate singers on their ability to sing expressive phrases, not on their ability to recognize dotted eighth note patterns. Maintain a consistency between what you are teaching and what you are grading.

In my value system, expectations for all are high, but no one who tries should fail; independent musicianship is highly valued; and respect of and encouragement among individuals is paramount.

My report card grade criteria might look like this:

50% Daily grades indicating improvement in skills
(based on individual assessment of daily activities)

25% Concert performances & evaluation of those performances
(the summative activity of all rehearsals)

25% Evidence of teamwork
(contributing to the group through attitude, behavior, supportive comments and actions, lack of negativity)

Some hints when developing a grading system.

- Make sure your system is consistent with the requirements of your school or district. If everyone else is required to have 12 grades per marking period, then you should too. It lends credibility to you and to our profession. If everyone is required to do writing across the curriculum, then you should too.
- Make sure you can live with your grading system. Make sure your system fits within your own value system.
- Do not rely on grades as motivation for effort or as punishment. "If you don't do this you will fail this class." only works with students who are motivated by grades and those may be the folks with whom you are not having trouble anyway.
- Make sure your system is fair to all concerned. Make your grading system public and tell students and their parents how singers will be evaluated and how it will benefit their vocal development. Be able to justify your grading decisions at all times.

Please see the references listed below for more information on grading.

Killian, Janice N. (January, 1999). The Grading Game. *VocalEase.* 4(1). 10-13.

Killian, Janice N. (1995). Assessment in Music Performing Groups: Some Practical Suggestions. In Christopher Doane (Ed.), *Proceedings of Suncoast Music Education Forum on Assessment.* Tampa: University of South Florida Press. http://arts.usf.edu/music/smef/art-jk.html

Matheny, John. (January, 1994). A grading system for secondary music groups. *Music Educators Journal.* 37-39.

MENC. (1998). *Teaching Music.* 6(2). Entire issue.

VOICE BUILDERS

Posture: Page 2
Breathing: Page 3

Lesson Objective:
The student is expected to master fundamental skills and basic performance techniques by demonstrating correct singing posture and breathing.

National Standard 1A:
Students sing accurately and with good breath control throughout their singing ranges, alone and in small and large ensembles.

Directions:
Posture: Page 2
Use the posture worksheet at various times throughout the year to:
- Identify steps of correct posture
- Remind students of correct posture
- Assess posture by means of self evaluation
- Grade students on posture (summative evaluation)

Breathing: Page 3
Use the breathing worksheet at various times throughout the year to:
- Identify characteristics of correct breathing
- Remind students to breathe correctly
- Self-evaluate breathing correctness
- Grade students on correct breathing (summative evaluation)
- Encourage students to do exercises at home.

Basic Vowels: Page 4

Lesson Objective:
The student is expected to master fundamental skills and basic performance techniques by demonstrating correct vowels.

National Standard 1A:
Students sing accurately and with good breath control throughout their singing ranges, alone and in small and large ensembles.

Directions:
Distribute copies of the Vowels Checklist to each student. Ask students to sing a familiar song or a familiar warm-up exercise while using correct vowel shapes. Slow sustained passages work best. Use the Vowel Checklist at various times throughout the year to:
- Identify correct vowel shapes
- Remind students of correct vowel shapes
- Allow students to self-evaluate correct vowel shapes
- Grade students on correct vowel shapes when singing an exercise
- Grade students on correct vowel shapes when singing a song

Diphthongs: Page 5

Lesson Objective:
The student is expected to demonstrate fundamental skills and basic performance techniques by developing and then demonstrating a knowledge of diphthongs.

National Standard 1A:
Students sing accurately and with good breath control throughout their singing ranges, alone and in small and large ensembles.

Directions:
Distribute copies of Diphthongs Checklist to each student. Follow written directions on the worksheet to emphasize the characteristics of diphthongs. Further information about diphthongs may be found in *Musicianship Level 2* (student book p. 118) and *Musicianship Level 3* (student book p. 180).

Answers:
1a. "eh" followed by "ee"
1b. "ah" followed by "ee"
1c. "oh" followed by "oo"
1d. "ah" followed by "oo"
1e. "oh" followed by "oo"
1f. "ah" followed by "ee"
1g. "ah" followed by "oo"
1h. "ee" followed by "oo"
2. Answers will vary.

Physiology Information: Page 6
Physiology Quiz: Page 7

Lesson Objective:
The student is expected to recognize and label the anatomy of the vocal mechanism.

National Standard 8B:
Students describe ways in which the principles and subject matter of other disciplines taught in the school are interrelated with those of music.

Directions:
Physiology Information: Page 6
Distribute copies of the Physiology Information Sheet to each student. Instruct them to read it carefully. You may want to discuss the physiology of the voice with them. Pull-apart plastic models of the vocal apparatus are helpful to demonstrate the various parts of the vocal mechanism. Another helpful tool is a video, *The Voice: Three Professionals Discuss the Function, Abuses and Care of the Most Important Instrument of Communication* by Charles Nelson, Austin King and Jon Ashby published by Voice Institute of West Texas at Abilene Christian University.

Physiology Quiz: Page 7
Distribute copies of the Physiology Quiz to each student. Ask them to label the parts of the breathing mechanism and the vocal mechanism. Use this as a practice worksheet or as a summative quiz. Further information may be found in *Musicianship Level 2* (student pp. 70 and 80) or *Musicianship Level 3* (student pp. 51 and 76).

Answers:
1. c **2.** b **3.** d **4.** e **5.** a **6.** a **7.** b **8.** c

THEORY BUILDERS

Level 1: Pages 8-14 Linked to *Musicianship Level 1*

Lesson Objective:
The student is expected to demonstrate fundamental skills in basic music theory.

National Standard 5C:
Students identify and define standard notation symbols for pitch, rhythm, dynamics, tempo, articulation and expression.

Directions:
Complete the lessons in *Musicianship Level 1* before completing the corresponding activity sheet.

1. Distribute appropriate theory Activity Sheet to students.
2. Discuss procedure as explained on sheet.
3. Allow students to complete the worksheet as a classroom activity or as homework.
4. Use the Activity Sheets as a practice open-book exercise or as a summative assessment activity.
5. Grade student work during or outside of class time.
6. Re-teach any material not mastered by the majority of the class.

Answers:

Page 8 Beat, Rhythm and Notation (EE 1 & 2)
1. Rhythm is the organization of sound length (duration). **2.** Beat is the steadily recurring pulse in music. **3.** See student page 19. **4a.** quarter rest **4b.** half rest **4c.** quarter rest **4d.** whole rest

Page 9 Meter (EE 3 & 4)
1. meter **2.** The top number indicates the number of beats per measure. **3.** The bottom number indicates what type of note gets the beat. **4.** 4 beats per measure and the quarter note receives the beat. **5.** 3 beats per measure and the quarter note receives the beat. **6.** 2 beats per measure and the quarter note receives the beat.

Page 10 Eighth and Sixteenth Notes (EE 5 & 6)
1. eighth note **2.** sixteenth note **3.** division of the beat **4.** subdivision of the beat **5a.** beat **5b.** division **5c.** subdivision

Page 11 Key Signature – F Major (EE 8 & 9)
1. key signature and keynote **2.** one; F **3a.** do, re, mi, fa, sol **3b.** do, ti, la, sol

Page 12 Ties, Slurs, and Dotted Quarter Notes (EE 12 & 13)
1. true **2.** false **3a.** tie **3b.** slur **3c.** tie **3d.** slur **4.** One half **5a.** true **5b.** true **5c.** false **5d.** true

Page 13 Syncopation and Compound Meter (EE 16 & 17)
1. accents and ties

Page 14 Finding the Major Key (EE 18)
1. Rule 1 – If there are no sharps or flats in the key signature, *do* is C. Rule 2 – If the key signature includes flats, the last flat (that is, the flat farthest to the right) is *fa.* Count up the scale five steps or down the scale four steps to find *do.* Rule 3 – If the key signature includes sharps, the last sharp (that is, the sharp farthest to the right) is *ti.* Count up the scale one step or down the scale seven steps to find *do.* **2a.** key of G major and the keynote is G **2b.** key of E major and the keynote is E **2c.** key of B♭ and the keynote is B♭

Level 2: Pages 15-26
Linked to
Musicianship Level 2

Lesson Objective:
The student is expected to demonstrate fundamental skills in basic music theory.

National Standard 5C:
Students identify and define standard notation symbols for pitch, rhythm, dynamics, tempo, articulation, and expression.

Directions:
Complete the materials and lessons in *Musicianship Level 2* before completing corresponding activity sheet.

1. Distribute appropriate Theory Activity Sheet to students.
2. Discuss procedure as explained on sheet.
3. Allow students to complete the worksheet as a classroom activity or as homework.
4. Use the Activity Sheets as a practice open-book activity or as a summative assessment activity.
5. Grade them during or outside of class time.
6. Reteach any material not mastered by the majority of the class.

Answers:

Page 15 Basic Rhythm Notation (EE1)
1. rhythm **2.** beat **3.** whole note, half note, quarter note **5a.** 5 **5b.** 10 **5c.** 9 **6a.** quarter note **6b.** half note **6c.** quarter note.

Page 16 Basic Pitch Notation – Treble Clef (EE2)
1. staff **2.** clef **3.** G **5.** Line Notes: C,E,G,B,D,F; Space Notes: D, F, A, C, E, G

Page 17 Basic Pitch Notation – Bass Clef (EE2)
1. 5 & 4 **2.** bass **3.** F **5.** Line Notes: G, B, D, F, A; Space Notes: A, C, E, G, B

Page 18 Musical Spelling (EE2)
1a. CABBAGE **1b.** DAD **3a.** BAGGAGE **3b.** CAB

Page 19 Meter and Time Signature (EE3)
1. C **2.** F **3.** E **4.** A **5.** D **6.** B **7.** 4, quarter **8.** 3, quarter **9.** 2, quarter **10.** quarter note and half note 11. quarter note and quarter note

Page 20 Meter and Time Signature – Part 2 (EE3)
1a. quarter note and half note **1b.** quarter note and half note

Page 21 Key of C Major (EE 5 & 6)
1. G **2.** F **3.** D **4.** A **5.** B **6.** E **7.** H **8.** C **9.** none (zero) **10.** C, D, E, F, G, A, B, C **11.** E & F; B & C.

Page 22 Key of G Major (EE 8 & 9)
1. accidental **2.** sharp **3.** flat **4.** interval **5.** G, A, B, C, D, E, F♯, G **6.** one sharp in key signature on F; keynote is G **7a.-7g.** W, W, H, W, W, W, H

Page 23 The "Rest" is Up to You! (EE 10 & 11)
1. rest **2a.** whole rest, 4 beats **2b.** half rest, 2 beats **2c.** quarter rest, 1 beat **4a.** quarter, half, half, half rest **4b.** quarter, quarter, quarter, half rest **5a.** 2 **5b.** 2 **5c.** 4

Page 24 Key of F Major (EE 16)
1. one **2.** LEFT **3.** F, G, A, B♭, C, D, E, F **4.** F, G, A, B♭, C, D, E, F **5.** one flat on B; keynote is F **6.** *pp, p, mp, mf, f, ff*.

Page 25 Rhythm Review – The Dot (EE 16)
1. half **2.** RIGHT **3.** whole note, dotted half note, half note, quarter note. **4.** Answers may vary. **5a.** 9 **5b.** 12

Page 26 Eighth Notes and Rests (EE 17-19)
1. 1/2 beats, 1/2 beats **2.** beamed and unbeamed **3.** Write 2 sets of beamed or 4 unbeamed notes **4a.** True **4b.** True **4c.** False **4d.** False **4e.** True **4f.** False **5a.** 4/4 **5b.** 2/4 **5c.** 4/4

Level 3: Pages 27-39 Linked to *Musicianship Level 3*

Lesson Objective:
The student is expected to demonstrate fundamental skills in intermediate music theory.

National Standard 5C:
Students identify and define standard notation symbols for pitch, rhythm, dynamics, tempo, articulation, and expression.

Directions:
Complete the materials and lessons in *Musicianship Level 3* before completing corresponding activity sheet.

1. Distribute appropriate Theory Activity Sheet to students.
2. Discuss procedure as explained on sheet.
3. Allow students to complete the worksheet as a classroom activity or as homework.
4. Use the Activity Sheets as a practice open-book activity or as a summative assessment activity.
5. Grade them during or outside of class time.
6. Reteach any material not mastered by the majority of the class.

Answers:

Page 27 Basic Rhythmic Notation (EE 1)
1. rhythm **2.** beat **3.** rest **4a.** whole note = 4 **4b.** half note = 2 **4c.** quarter = 1 **4d.** whole rest = 4 **4e.** half rest = 2 **4f.** quarter rest = 1 **5.** 2 **6.** 2 **7.** 4 **8.** 2 **9a.** 5 **9b.** 6

Page 28 Basic Rhythmic Notation – Part 2 (EE 1)
1a. quarter note **1b.** half note **1c.** half note **1d.** quarter note **1e.** half note **1f.** whole note **2a.** quarter, half, half rests **2b.** quarter, quarter, quarter rest **2c.** quarter, none, quarter rests **2d.** quarter, half, half, whole rests

Page 29 Basic Pitch Notation – Bass Clef (EE 1)
1. staff **2.** 5 & 4 **3.** grand staff **4.** treble clef **5.** bass clef **6.** G **7.** F **8.** Line Notes: C, E, G, B, D, F; Space Notes: D, F, A, C, E, G **9.** Line Notes: G, B, D, F, A; Space Notes: A, C, E, G, B

Page 30 Musical Spelling (EE 1)
1a. CAGE **1b.** FACE **2a.** ADDED **2b.** ACE **3a.** BAGGAGE **3b.** BAG **3c.** BADGE **3d.** CAFE

Page 31 Meter and Time Signature – (EE 2 & 8)
1. E **2.** F **3.** D **4.** B **5.** C **6.** A **7.** 4, quarter **8.** 3, quarter **9.** 2, quarter **10.** half note and quarter note **11.** quarter note and quarter note

Page 32 Meter and Time Signature – Part 2 (EE 2 & 8)
1a. quarter, quarter, half note **1b.** quarter, half, half note

Page 33 Key of C Major (EE 2 & 3)
1. I **2.** F **3.** J **4.** A **5.** B **6.** E **7.** H **8.** C **9.** G **10.** D **11.** C, D, E, F, G, A, B, C **12a.-12g.** W, W, H, W, W, W, H

Page 34 Key of G Major (EE 4)
1. accidental **2.** sharp **3.** flat **4.** G, A, B, C, D, E, F♯, G **5.** one sharp in key signature on F; keynote is G **6a.-6g.** W, W, H, W, W, W, H

Page 35 Intervals (EE5)
1. interval **2.** melodic **3.** harmonic **4a.** 5th **4b.** 3rd **4c.** 4th **4d.** octave **4e.** 2nd **5a.** 5th **5b.** 3rd **5c.** 2nd **5d.** 5th **5e.** 6th **5f.** 6th **6a.** C **6b.** E **6c.** B **6d.** E **6e.** F **7a.** E **7b.** G **7c.** A **7d.** D **7e.** G **7f.** B

Page 36 Key of F Major (EE 12)
1. F, G, A, B♭, C, D, E, F **2a-2g.** W, W, H, W, W, W, H **3.** one **4.** 3rd line **5.** 2nd line **6a.** tonic (I) **6b.** dominant (V)

Page 37 Key of D Major (EE 14)
1. D, E, F♯, G, A, B, C♯, D **2.** two sharps (F♯, C♯); keynote is G. **3a.** tonic (I) **3b.** subdominant (IV) **3c.** dominant (V)

Page 38 Key of B♭ Major (EE 17)
1. two **2.** B and E **3.** B♭, C, D, E♭, F, G, A, B♭ **4.** two flats (B♭ and E♭); keynote is B♭ **5a.** Tonic (I) **5b.** subdominant (IV) **5c.** dominant (V)

Page 39 Rhythm Practice (EE 9 & 15)
1. 1/2 **2.** beamed and unbeamed **3.** beamed and unbeamed **4.** See chapters 9 and 15 for answer **5a.** False **5b.** False **5c.** False **5d.** True **5e.** True **5f.** True **6.** Answers will vary **7.** Apply your own counting system.

Level 4: Pages 40-52 Linked to *Musicianship Level 4*

Lesson Objective:
The student is expected to demonstrate fundamental skills in advanced music theory.

National Standard 5C:
Students identify and define standard notation symbols for pitch, rhythm, dynamics, tempo, articulation, and expression.

Directions:
Complete the materials and lessons in *Musicianship Level 4* before completing corresponding activity sheet.

1. Distribute appropriate Theory Activity Sheet to students.
2. Discuss procedure as explained on sheet.
3. Allow students to complete the worksheet as a classroom activity or as homework.
4. Use the Activity Sheets as a practice open-book activity or as a summative assessment activity.
5. Grade them during or outside of class time.
6. Reteach any material not mastered by the majority of the class.

Answers:

Page 40 Relative Minor Scale (EE 1)
1. tonic **2.** half **3.** whole **4.** key **5.** 6th **6.** A, B, C, D, E, F, G, A **7a.** B & C **7b.** E & F **8.** Half steps in the major scale occur between steps 3 & 4 and 7 & 8. Half steps in the relative minor scale occur between steps 2 & 3 and 5 & 6.

Page 41 Relative Minor Scales, Part 2 (EE 1)
1a. C major, A minor **1b.** G major, E minor **1c.** B♭ major, G minor **1d.** A major, F# minor **2.** C minor scale: C, D, E♭, F, G, A♭, B♭, C; half steps between D & E♭ and G & A♭

Page 42 Rhythmic Notation (EE 2)
1. meter **2.** time signature **3a.** 3, eighth **3b.** 2, quarter **3c.** 3, half **4.** See text (EE2) for more information

Page 43 Intervals (EE 3 & 4)
1. interval **2.** melodic **3.** harmonic **4a.** major **4b.** minor **4c.** perfect **4d.** diminished **5a.** M3 **5b.** P4 **5c.** P5 **5d.** M6 **5e.** M7 **5f.** P8 **6a.** m3 **6b.** P4 **6c.** P5 **6d.** m6 **6e.** m7 **6f.** P8

Page 44 Intervals, Part 2 (EE 3 & 4)
1a. minor **1b.** augmented **1c.** diminished **1d.** augmented **2a.** example **2b.** change A to A♭ **2c.** change B to B♭ **2d.** change F♯ to F-natural **3a.** change B to B♭ **3b.** change D to D♯ **3c.** change G to G♭ **3d.** change A♭ to A double flat.

Page 45 Categories of Harmony (EE 5-7)
1. dominant, major, V; leading tone, dimished vii°; mediant, minor, iii; supertonic, minor, ii; subdominant, major, IV; submediant, minor, vi **2.** I, IV, V, I **3.** I, ii, V, I

Page 46 Categories of Harmony, Part 2 (EE 5-7)
1a. triads built on C, F, G **1b.** triads built on E♭, G, C, E♭ **1c.** triads built on G, A, C, D **1d.** triads built on F, G, C, E **2a.** I, vi, IV, V **2b.** I, iii, vii°, IV **2c.** I, V, ii, IV

Page 47 Compound Meter (EE 8)
1. time signature **2.** compound **3.** compound **4a.-4f.** True, True, False, False, True, True **5a.** 3, quarter, simple **5b.** 12, eighth, compound **5c.** 8, quarter, simple **5d.** 9, quarter, compound **5e.** 6, quarter, compound **5f.** 6, eighth, compound.

Page 48 Compound Meter, Part 2 (EE 8)
Answers may vary. Consult text.

Page 49 Accidentals (EE 13)
1. natural **2.** chromatic **3.** diatonic **4a.** D **4b.** C **4c.** D **4d.** C **4e.** D **5a.** C **5b.** B♭ **5c.** F♯ **5d.** E-natural

Page 50 Diatonic/Chromatic Scales (EE 13)
1. diatonic, different **2.** The major scale **3.** D, E, F♯, G, A, B, C♯, D **4.** half **5.** octave **6.** A(♭), A-natural, B(♭), B-natural, C, C♯, D, E(♭), E-natural, F, F♯, G, A(♭)

Page 51 Harmonic/Melodic Minor Scales (EE 14)
1a. natural **1b.** harmonic **1c.** melodic **2.** harmonic **3.** 6th & 7th **4.** A, B, C, D, E, F, G, A **5.** Place a sharp sign before G and A ascending. Return to G and A natural descending. Ascending steps: W, H, W, W, W, W, H. Descending steps: W, W, H, W, W, H, W.

Page 52 Asymmetric Meter (EE 17)
1. meter **2.** time signature **3.** asymmetrical **4a.** 2, quarter, simple **4b.** 5, quarter, asymmetric **4c.** 6, eighth, compound **4d.** 7, eighth, asymmetric **5.** Consult text **6.** Creations will vary.

SIGHT-READING • MELODIC

Level 1: Page 53
Linked to
Musicianship Level 1

Lesson Objective:
The student is expected to demonstrate individual fundamental skills in melodic sight-reading through prepared assessment exercises.

National Standard 5B:
Students read at sight simple melodies in both the treble and bass clefs.

Level 2: Pages 54-56
Linked to
Musicianship Level 2

Lesson Objective:
The student is expected to demonstrate individual fundamental skills in melodic sight-reading through prepared assessment exercises.

National Standard 5B:
Students read at sight simple melodies in both the treble and bass clefs.

Level 3: Pages 57-59
Linked to
Musicianship Level 3

Lesson Objective:
The student is expected to demonstrate individual fundamental skills in melodic sight-reading through prepared assessment exercises.

National Standard 5B:
Students read at sight simple melodies in both the treble and bass clefs.

Level 4: Pages 60-62
Linked to
Musicianship Level 4

Lesson Objective:
The student is expected to demonstrate individual skills in melodic/rhythmic sight-reading through prepared assessment exercises.

National Standard 5B:
Students read at sight simple melodies in both the treble and bass clefs.

Directions:
The key is to have students perform these tests individually. The exercises appear to be simple, but individual sight reading is a complex task involving many skills. Therefore, keep individual tests simpler than group ones so that the students will experience some measure of success.

Possible uses for these exercises:
1. Pre-testing. Ask students to read as many exercises down the page as they can without making a mistake. It should give you a good assessment of the level of mastery for each individual student in your class.
2. Post-testing. Each exercise is linked to a specific chapter in *Musicianship Level 1, 2, 3, or 4*. Use the exercise as a summative activity to demonstrate mastery of the skills presented in that chapter.
3. Select specific exercises to serve as a testing tool for each grading period of the school year.
4. Re-write these exercises to meet your specific needs.
5. Make up your own sight reading exercises
   - Using short excerpts from the music you are currently studying in class.
   - Incorporating a concept, rhythm pattern or key you are currently studying.
   - Offering greater challenges to the more advanced student.
   - Providing easier examples for the struggling student.

Suggestions on assessment techniques.

A. **Individual taped testing**
   - The first student on the list goes into a practice room (hallway, etc) with tape recorder and records his/her name and sings the designated exercise. The student returns to rehearsal and hands the laminated list of names to the next person on the list; that person leaves to record; class rehearsal continues as usual. You, the teacher, then listen to and evaluate recorded exercises outside of class time. Share the results with each individual student.
   - Encourage students to come before or after school or during activity/ lunch hour to record their sight-reading tests.

B. **Classroom testing**
   Individuals sight-read while the group listens. Test only a few individuals on any given day to save time. You grade them as they sing so no further time is required on your part. For security with beginners, pairs of students may sing together on the same exercise. Graduate from this system in a hurry so that you can truly hear individuals.

SIGHT-READING • RHYTHM

Level 1: Page 63 Linked to *Musicianship Level 1*

Lesson Objective:
The student is expected to demonstrate individual rhythm reading skills on a beginning level through prepared assessment exercises.

National Standard 5A:
Students will read whole, half, quarter, eighth, sixteenth, and dotted notes and rests in various meter signatures.

Level 2: Page 64 Linked to *Musicianship Level 2*

Lesson Objective:
The student is expected to demonstrate individual rhythm reading skills on a beginning level through prepared assessment exercises.

National Standard 5A:
Students will read whole, half, quarter, eighth, sixteenth, and dotted notes and rests in various meter signatures.

Level 3: Page 65 Linked to *Musicianship Level 3*

Lesson Objective:
The student is expected to demonstrate individual rhythm reading skills on an intermediate level through prepared assessment exercises.

National Standard 5A:
Students will read whole, half, quarter, eighth, sixteenth, and dotted notes and rests in various meter signatures.

Level 4: Page 66 Linked to *Musicianship Level 4*

Lesson Objective:
The student is expected to demonstrate individual rhythm reading skills on an advanced level through prepared assessment exercises.

National Standard 5A:
Students will read whole, half, quarter, eighth, sixteenth, and dotted notes and rests in various meter signatures.

Directions:
The key is to have students perform these tests individually. The exercises appear to be simple, but individual rhythm reading is a challenging task. Therefore, keep individual tests simpler than group ones so that the students will experience some measure of success.

Possible uses for these exercises:

1. Pre-testing. Ask students to read as many exercises down the page as they can without making a mistake. It should give you a good assessment of the level of mastery for each individual student in your class.
2. Post-testing. Each exercise is linked to a specific chapter in *Musicianship Level 1, 2, 3, or 4*. Use the exercise as a summative activity to demonstrate mastery of the skills presented in that chapter.
3. Select specific exercises to serve as a testing tool for each grading period of the school year.
4. Re-write these exercises to meet your specific needs.
5. Make up your own sight-reading exercises
   - Using short excerpts from the music you are currently studying in class.
   - Incorporating a concept, rhythm pattern or key you are currently studying.
   - Offering greater challenges to the more advanced student.
   - Providing easier examples for the struggling student.

Suggestions on assessment techniques.

A. Individual taped testing.

- The first student on the list goes into a practice room (hallway, etc.) with tape recorder and records his/her name and taps/counts the designated exercise. The student returns to rehearsal and hands the laminated list of names to the next person on the list; that person leaves to record; class rehearsal continues as usual. You, the teacher, then listens to and evaluates recorded exercises outside of class time. Share the results with each individual student.
- Encourage students to come before or after school or doing activity/lunch hour to record their rhythm reading tests.

B. Classroom testing

Individuals rhythm read while the group listens. Test only a few individuals on any given day to save time. You grade them as they sing and so no further time is required on your part. For security with beginners, pairs of students may tap/count/chant/conduct together on the same exercise. Graduate from this system in a hurry so that you can truly hear individuals.

C. Conducting

Another effective way to assess rhythmic reading is to teach students to conduct and count out loud. Always remember that the conducting beat should remain steady. The point is to feel the steady pulse, not merely perform the conducting pattern. Strive for steadiness without beat hesitations. As they become more proficient with reading and conducting, have each student perform the rhythm exercises individually for a grade.

REHEARSAL TECHNIQUES

Tone Quality – Part 1 and 2: Pages 68 and 69

Lesson Objective:
The student is expected to identify and practice effective tone quality by comparing their own tone with contrasting descriptors.

National Standard 6A:
Students describe specific musical events in a given aural example, using appropriate terminology.

Directions:

1. Prior to doing this activity, ask volunteers to record a familiar song such as *My Country Tis of Thee.* This will give you a sound bank of unnamed individual voices for the class to analyze as an introduction to this worksheet.
2. Distribute copies of the Tone Quality Descriptors to each student. It is recommended that you use Part 1 for basic level and Part 2 for advanced level.
3. Make sure students understand the concept of tone quality (timbre).
4. Listen to the recording. Analyze tone quality using the descriptors.
5. Ask students to use Tone Quality Descriptors in a variety of ways.
   - Analyze tone quality using a recording of their own solo voice
   - Analyze tone quality using a recording of their entire choir
   - Analyze tone quality after a rehearsal (no recording)
   - Compare results as a cooperative learning project
6. Use the Tone Quality Descriptors at various times throughout the year to emphasize the development of tone quality.

Balance and Blend– Part 1 and Part 2: Pages 70 and 71

Lesson Objective:
The student is expected to identify and practice appropriate balance and blend by completing a worksheet indicating their understanding of balance and blend in a choral setting.

National Standard 6A:
Students describe specific musical events in a given aural example, using appropriate terminology.

Directions:

1. Make sure students understand the concept of blend and balance.
2. Distribute copies of the Blend and Balance to each student. It is recommended that you use Part 1 for basic level and Part 2 for advanced level.

Answers:
Page 70 Balance and Blend, Part 1
1. T **2.** T **3.** T **4.** T

Page 71 Balance and Blend, Part 2
1. There are exceptions. Balance does not always mean equal loudness among sections. For example, if the altos have the melody they should probably be louder than the rest of the choir. Polyphonic entrances should be emphasized so the entering voice part should be slightly louder than the rest of the choir. **2.** Soloists should usually be louder than other singers in the choir.

Diction • Languages: Page 72

Lesson Objective:
The student is expected to demonstrate fundamental skills and basic performance techniques by demonstrating correct diction.

National Standard 1A:
Students sing accurately and with good breath control throughout their singing ranges, alone and in small and large ensembles.

Directions:
1. Distribute copies of the Diction • Languages Descriptors to each student.
2. Ask students to use Diction • Language Descriptors in a variety of ways.
   - Analyze diction or language using a recording of their own solo voice
   - Analyze diction or language using a recording of their entire choir
3. Use the Diction • Language Descriptors at various times throughout the year to emphasize the development of diction and foreign language.

Interpretation: Page 73

Lesson Objective:
The student is expected to identify and practice effective singing by analyzing expressive techniques used by the choir.

National Standard 1B:
Students sing with expression and technical accuracy.

Directions:
1. Distribute copies of the Interpretation worksheet to each student.
2. Listen to a recording of the choir. Use the Interpretation worksheet to analyze dynamics, phrasing, following composer markings, etc.
3. Ask students to compare answers in a collaborative learning environment.

Note: Less experienced singers may be more successful considering only dynamics. If so, use only the top half of the checklist (Questions 1-4).

4. Use the Interpretation Checklist at various times throughout the year to emphasize the development of sensitivity to expressive aspects of music.

Ensemble Precision: Page 74

Lesson Objective:
The student is expected to identify and practice effective precision techniques.

National Standard 1B:
Students sing with expression and technical accuracy.

Directions:
This form may be used in two ways. Option 1 is to have students reflect on a prior performance with answers based on what they perceived they heard or did. Option 2 is to have students analyze a video or audio recording of a prior performance.

1. Distribute copies of the Precision Chart to each student.
2. Use the Precision Chart to analyze attacks, releases, vowels, rhythm and pitch accuracy.
3. Ask students to compare answers in a collaborative learning environment.
4. Use the Precision Chart at various times throughout the year to emphasize the development of accurate and precise choral singing.

Physical Involvement • Attentiveness: Page 75

Lesson Objective:
Students are expected to identify and practice appropriate physical involvement by analyzing their own movement, facial expression and attentiveness.

National Standard 6A:
Students describe specific musical events in a given aural example, using appropriate terminology.

Directions:

1. Distribute copies of the Physical Involvement • Attentiveness Checklist to each student. The checklist may be used several ways:
    - Video the choir and ask students to complete the Physical Involvement • Attentiveness Checklist regarding the entire choir.
    - Video the choir and ask students to complete the Physical Involvement • Attentiveness Checklist regarding their own contribution.
    - Ask students to complete the checklist as they reflect on their physical involvement (no taping).
2. Less experienced singers may be more successful emphasizing only facial expression and eye motion. If so, use only questions 1 and 2.
3. Use the Physical Involvement • Attentiveness Checklist at various times throughout the year to emphasize the importance of appropriate movement in an excellent choir.

Attentiveness • Behavior Expectations: Page 76

Lesson Objective:
The student is expected to identify and practice appropriate and effective rehearsal techniques.

National Standard 7B:
Students evaluate the quality and effectiveness of their own ... performances by applying ... constructive suggestions for improvement.

Directions:
Distribute copies of the Attentiveness • Behavior Expectations Checklist to each student. Use the Checklist at various times throughout the year:

- Prior to rehearsal to reinforce your chosen rehearsal procedures (results not graded; each student completes his or her own checklist)
- To check skills (results not graded; each student completes his or her own checklist)
- After a rehearsal throughout the year as a reminder of expectations
- After a rehearsal as a summative evaluation (results graded)
- During a rehearsal as an evaluation of an individual student's attentiveness. Individual student completes his or her checklist. A classroom observer completes checklist on the same individual student. Compare results of individual student self-assessment with observer assessment.

PERFORMANCE EVALUATION

Performance Evaluations: Pages 77 to 82

Lesson Objective:
The student is expected to identify and practice appropriate and effective performance techniques.

National Standard 7A & 7B:
Students develop criteria for evaluating the quality and effectiveness of music performances and apply that criteria in their personal performing ... and offer constructive suggestions for improvement.

Directions:

1. Distribute copies of the appropriate Performance Assessment Checklists or Essays. Use the Checklists and Essays to evaluate performances at various times throughout the year.
2. Note: Inexperienced singers may have difficulty completing entire checklists. Consider using only a portion of each checklist until singers are familiar with self-evaluation procedures.
3. Complete Checklists and/or Essays in a variety of ways:
   - Evaluating after viewing a video or audio of a recent concert
   - Evaluating after reflecting on a recent concert in which the singers were concert participants
   - Evaluating after reflecting on a recent concert in which the singers were the audience
4. Note: Comparing evaluations among choir members is an excellent exercise in discussing the subjectivity of evaluations/contests/judging, etc. This procedure is also an excellent way to involve students in collaborative learning.

CONCERT ETIQUETTE

Concert Etiquette Information: Page 83

Concert Etiquette Quiz: Page 84 and 85

Lesson Objective:
The student is expected to demonstrate an understanding of proper concert etiquette.

National Standard 7A:
Students develop criteria for evaluating the quality and effectiveness of music performances and compositions and apply the criteria in their personal listening and performing.

Directions:

1. Distribute copies of Concert Etiquette activity sheets to students.
2. Read, review, and discuss the material presented on Concert Etiquette Information sheet.
3. When you feel students are adequately prepared, give them the Concert Etiquette Quiz found on Pages 84 or 85.
4. You may use this quiz as a class or group activity or as an individual assessment tool.

Answers:
Page 84 Concert Etiquette Quiz, Basic
1. F **2.** T **3.** F **4.** T **5.** F **6.** T **7.** F **8.** T **9.** F **10.** T **11-13.** Answers may vary. Accept reasonable responses.

Page 85 Concert Etiquette Quiz, Advanced
1. c **2.** d **3.** d **4.** Answers may vary. Some acceptable answers would be to not distract performers on stage or other members of the audience; to insure a better performance; to not embarrass yourself with inappropriate behavior; to show respect for the performers and appreciate the time and effort they gave in preparing for the performance; to display good manners **5.** Answers may vary. Discuss appropriate behavior reacting to inappropriate audience behavior. **6.** Answers may vary. Class discussion.

MUSIC HISTORY

Lesson Objective:
The student is expected to know characteristics of music from the specified historical period and identify characteristics of that era music by listening to exemplary examples from that era.

National Standard 9B:
Students classify by genre, style, historical period, composer, and title a varied body of exemplary musical works and explain the characteristics that cause each work to be considered exemplary.

Materials:
Copies of the Time Line, Characteristics Lesson, and Quiz of the historical period to be studied.
Teacher Resource Kit Listening CD

Procedure:

1. Give students enough time to read Time Line and Characteristics Lesson. Use discussion, group work, silent reading or any other variety of presentation method.
2. Play specified recording. Multiple listenings may be needed.
3. Answer questions on lesson activity page.
4. Give appropriate quiz as a formative activity (open book or discussion) or as a summative activity (graded test after historical period material has been mastered).

Middle Ages Era Listening: Pages 87 to 89

Alma Redemptoris Mater by Palestrina, *Listening CD*, Track 1

Glorificamus te by Butler, *Listening CD*, Track 2

Answers:
Page 88, Middle Ages Era Characteristics
1. Beginning **2.** Middle – towards the end
3. & 4. All except monophonic singing, Latin text
5. Answers may vary. Open ended question.

Page 89, Middle Ages Era Quiz
1. B **2.** A **3.** C **4.** C **5.** A **6.** See Timeline
7. Open discussion

Renaissance Era Listening: Pages 90 to 92

Alma Redemptoris Mater by Palestrina, *Listening CD*, Track 1

Answers:
Page 91, Renaissance Era Characteristics
1. A cappella, sacred text, Latin. **2.** Sounds mostly hymn-like, Sounds like a piece sung by men and women, Latin text. **3.** Answers are subjective and open-ended.

Page 92, Renaissance Era Quiz
1. B **2.** C **3.** A **4.** C **5.** B **6.** A **7.** B **8.** See Renaissance Time Line **9.** Subjective open-ended answers

Baroque Era Listening: Pages 93 to 95

Let the Whole Earth Stand in Awe by Handel, *Listening CD*, Track 3

Answers:
Page 94, Baroque Era Characteristics
1. T **2.** F **3.** T **4.** T **5.** F **6.** Extended Listening: For the most part it has a continuously moving accompaniment. Exceptions – beginning and ending.

Enrichment: Listen to other Baroque works and try this same checklist.

Page 95, Baroque Era Quiz
1. C **2.** A **3.** B **4.** A **5.** B **6.** B **7.** *Sound the Trumpet* – Purcell (C) *Messiah* – Handel (D) *Gloria* – Vivaldi (B) *Christmas Oratorio* – Bach (A) **8.** See Baroque Time Line **9.** Rubens – painter Cervantes – author of *Don Quixote*; Defoe – author of *Robinson Crusoe*; Swift – author of *Gulliver's Travels*

Classical Era Listening: Pages 96 to 98

 *Gloria* (from *Heiligmesse*) by Haydn, *Listening CD*, Track 4

 *Gloria in Excelsis* (from *Gloria*) by Vivaldi, *Listening CD*, Track 5

Answers:

Page 97, Classical Era Characteristics

Haydn – Classical: Check all items *except* elaborate ornamentation, accompaniment steady 8th notes throughout

Vivaldi – Baroque: Check all items *except* tuneful melody, accompaniment patterns change

Page 98, Classical Era Quiz

1. A **2.** A **3.** C **4.** B **5.** C **6.** B **7.** See Classical Time Line **8.** A **9.** *Candide* – Voltaire (C), *Faust* – Goethe (D), Dictionary – Johnson (A), *Pride and Prejudice* – Jane Austen (B) **10.** Wordsworth – poet; Napoleon-political leader of France

Romantic Era Listening: Pages 99 to 101

 *In Praise of Spring* by Mendelssohn, *Listening CD*, Track 6

Answers:

Page 100, Romantic Era Characteristics

1. Soprano **2.** True **3.** 4 **4.** Thick **5.** Refer to Romantic Characteristics

Page 101, Romantic Era Quiz

1. A **2.** C **3.** B **4.** A **5.** C **6.** A **7.** See Romantic Era Time Line. Open discussion.

Twentieth Century Era Listening: Pages 102 to 104

 *Praise the Name of God with a Song* by Koepke, *Listening CD*, Track 7

 *Glorificamus te* by Butler, *Listening CD*, Track 2

Answers:

Page 103, Twentieth Century Characteristics

1. *Praise the Name of God with a Song* – check all boxes except Gregorian chant, uses female voices, and uses ancient text; *Glorificamus te* – check all boxes except uses male/female voices, includes aleatoric passages **2.** Open-ended answer.

Page 104, Twentieth Century Quiz

1. A **2.** A **3.** C **4.** B **5.** C **6.** *Great Gatsby*, Fitzgerald (B); *Grapes of Wrath* – Steinbach (C); *For Whom the Bell Tolls* – Hemingway (A) **7. & 8.** See Twentieth Century Timeline. **9.** Answers will vary. Encourage discussion.

LISTENING LESSONS 

Polyphonic Entrances: Page 106

Lesson Objective:
The student is expected to accurately identify polyphonic entrances.

National Standard 6A:
Students describe specific musical events in a given aural example, using appropriate terminology.

Materials:
 *Psallite* by Praetorius, *Listening CD*, Track 8

Directions:
Distribute copies of Polyphonic Entrances activity sheet.

1. Read and discuss the worksheet info about the composer and the times.
2. Play the opening of *Psallite* as many times as necessary for singers to answer the first question. Multiple listenings may be needed.
3. Discuss answers.
4. Listen to all of *Psallite* to answer questions 2-3.
5. Share responses to the final question.

Answers:
1. different times **2.** Soprano – 3, Alto – 4, Tenor – 1, Bass – 2 **3.** polyphonic **4.** Answers may vary. Discuss student choices. **5.** What instruments? Artist performing? Style? Tempo? Discuss all possibilities.

Unison • Harmony: Page 107

Lesson Objective:
The student is expected to aurally identify and distinguish unison from harmony in a choral setting.

National Standard 6A:
Students describe specific musical events in a given aural example, using appropriate terminology.

Materials:
 *Make a Song for My Heart to Sing* by Knowles, *Listening CD*, Track 9

Directions:

1. Distribute copies of Unison • Harmony activity sheet
2. Read and discuss the background information on the Unison • Harmony activity sheet.
3. Play the opening of Make a *Song for My Heart to Sing* and discuss the answers to Question 1. Multiple listenings may be necessary.

Answers:
1. Unison **2.** Harmony **3.** Unison **4.** Harmony **5.** Harmony

Extension: Discuss pattern seen in Questions 1-5. Usually the verse is in unison and the refrain is in harmony, except for the last verse, which is in harmony.

Who Has the Melody?: Page 108

Lesson Objective:
The student is expected to aurally identify and distinguish between melody and harmony.

National Standard 6A:
Students describe specific musical events in a given aural example, using appropriate terminology.

Materials:

Cripple Creek arr. by Crocker,
Listening CD, Track 10

Directions:

1. Distribute copies of Who Has the Melody? activity sheet.
2. Read and discuss information on activity sheet.
3. Play the opening of *Cripple Creek* and discuss the answers to 1 and 2 as a class.
4. Listen to all of *Cripple Creek* to answer questions 3-27. Multiple listenings may be necessary.
5. For less experienced listeners, it may be advisable to stop the CD after each verse and replay it to that point or simply pause for students to have time to write answers.
6. Suggested stopping spots: Stop after questions 1-4; 5-8; 9-11; 12-15; 16-19; 20-23; 24-27.

Answers:
1. Part I **2.** Part II **3.** Part I **4.** Part II **5.** Part I **6.** Part II **7.** Part I **8.** Part II **9.** Part I **10.** Part II **11.** Part I &II **12.** Part I **13.** Part II **14.** Part I **15.** Part II **16-19.** both parts equal **20.** Part I **21.** Part II **22.** Part I **23.** Part II **24-27.** both parts equal.

Dynamic Contrast: Page 109

Lesson Objective:
The student is expected to aurally identify and distinguish dynamic contrasts in a choral piece.

National Standard 6A:
Students describe specific musical events in a given aural example, using appropriate terminology.

Materials:

Charlotte-Town arr. by Crocker,
Listening CD, Track 11

Directions:

1. Distribute copies of Dynamic Contrasts activity Sheet.
2. Read and discuss the information on the activity sheet.
3. Play the opening of *Charlotte-Town* and discuss the answers to Question 1 as a class. Multiple listenings may be necessary.
4. Listen to the first three verses of *Charlotte-Town* to answer the rest of the questions.
5. For less experienced listeners, it may be advisable to stop the CD after each verse and replay it to that point or simply pause for students to have time to write answers.
6. Suggested stopping spots: Stop after questions 1; 2-5; 6-9; 10-13;

Answers:
1. forte **2.** forte **3.** forte **4.** piano **5.** forte **6.** forte **7.** forte **8.** piano **9.** forte **10.** forte **11.** piano **12.** forte **13.** piano.

Extension Activity: Change the following answers only. **3.** mezzo forte **4.** mezzo piano **7.** mezzo forte **8.** mezzo piano

Listening for Form – Strophic: Page 110

Lesson Objective:
The student is expected to discriminate between the repetition and contrast (form) of phrases in *Cripple Creek* and identify that form as strophic.

National Standard 6A:
Students describe specific musical events in a given aural example, using appropriate terminology.

Materials:

Cripple Creek arr. by Crocker,
Listening CD, Track 10

Directions:
1. Distribute copies of Listening for Form: Strophic activity sheet
2. Read and discuss the instructions on the worksheet. Listen to the opening of *Cripple Creek* and label the first two sections as "A" and "B" with the class as noted on the activity sheet. Discuss.
3. Play the entire song *Cripple Creek*. Continue to label each section as A or B. Multiple listenings will be necessary.
4. Emphasize that the challenge of listening for form is to remember what you've heard earlier and be able to identify whether it is the same or different from what you are hearing now.
5. After completing Question 1 and 2, instruct students to complete Questions 3-8.
6. Extension:
   A. Ask students to identify other works they are singing which are in strophic form.
   B. Ask students to identify and perhaps bring to class recordings of popular songs that are in strophic form.

Answers:
1. A **2.** B **3.** A **4.** B **5.** A **6.** B **7.** B **8.** Coda **9.** ABABABB Coda **10.** B sections have same music and same words **11a.** yes **11b.** Chorus **12a.** Yes **12b.** Strophic form is a musical form in which two different sections alternate. "A" section has the same music but different words; "B" section has the same words and music each time.

Listening for Form – ABA Form: Page 111

Lesson Objective:
The student is expected to discriminate between the repetition and contrast (form) of phrases in *Psallite* and identify that form as ABA.

National Standard 6A:
Students describe specific musical events in a given aural example, using appropriate terminology.

Materials:

Psallite by Praetorius,
Listening CD, Track 8

Directions:
1. Distribute copies of Listening for Form: ABA activity sheet.
2. Read and discuss the information on the activity sheet.
3. Play the entire song *Psallite* asking students to listen for the 3 sections.
4. Play the song again and ask students to raise their hands when they hear the end of the first section.
5. Stop and answer questions 1-2. Discuss responses. Emphasize that the challenge of listening for form is to remember what you've heard earlier and be able to identify whether it is the same or different from what you are hearing now.
6. Listen to all of *Psallite*. Thoughtful repeated listenings may be necessary.
7. Answer questions 3-7.
8. Extension: Ask students to identify other works they are singing which are in ABA form.

Answers:
1. Yes **2.** The entire choir pauses for a breath **3.** Different **4.** No **5.** Answers will vary **6.** Praetorius overlapped the start of the 3rd section with the ending of the 2nd section **7.** Yes

Listening for Form – Repetition of Sections: Page 112

Lesson Objective:
The student is expected to discriminate between the repetition and contrast (form) of phrases in *Ju Me Leve un Bel Maitín (In the Morning I Arose)* and expand his or her knowledge of form.

National Standard 6A:
Students describe specific musical events in a given aural example, using appropriate terminology.

Materials:

Ju Me Leve un Bel Maitín ed. Goodale, *Listening CD*, Track 12

Directions:

1. Distribute copies of Listening for Form: Repetition of Sections activity sheet.
2. Read and discuss the information on the activity sheet.
3. Listen to the entire song *Je Me Leve un Bel Maitín.*
4. On second listening, instruct students to raise their hands when they hear the end of a section and to think about how they know it is the end of a section.
5. Stop and answer Question 1. Discuss responses. Emphasize that the challenge of listening for form is to remember what you've heard earlier and be able to identify whether it is the same or different from what you are hearing now.
6. While listening to all *of Je Me Leve un Bel Maitín* again, ask students to answer Question 2. Thoughtful repeated listenings may be necessary.

Answers:
1. There is a pause (a fermata) at the end of each phrase **2.** A B C C C A A **3.** ABCCCAA

Listening for Balance: Page 113

Lesson Objective:
The student is expected to aurally identify appropriate balance among voice parts.

National Standard 6A:
Students describe specific musical events in a given aural example, using appropriate terminology.

Materials:

O occhi manza mia by di Lasso, *Listening CD*, Track 13 and Track 14

Directions:

1. Distribute copies of Listening for Balance activity sheet.
2. Read and discuss the definition of balance.
3. Answer Question 1.
4. Play the opening of *O occhi manza mia* Full Performance, Track 13 for singers and answer Question 3. Encourage them to answer with their first impression.
5. Listen to all of Full Performance, Track 13.
6. Now play Part-Learning, Track 14 and ask students to answer Question 4.
7. Complete Questions 5 and 6.

Answers:
All answers to this worksheet are subjective and may vary from person to person. The purpose of the worksheet is to consider the issue of balance and what our ears perceive as correct. This worksheet was not designed to be graded.

Spirituals Old and New: Page 114

Lesson Objective:
The student is expected to compare and contrast the musical and emotional characteristics of two spirituals (*Steal Away* and *Elijah Rock*).

National Standard 9A:
Students describe distinguishing characteristics of representative music genres and styles from a variety of cultures.

Materials:

 *Steal Away* arr. Bartholomew, *Listening CD*, Track 15

 *Elijah Rock* arr. Hogan, *Listening CD*, Track 16

Directions:

1. Distribute copies of the Listening to Spirituals Old and New activity sheet.
2. Read and discuss the worksheet information.
3. Play the opening of *Steal Away* and *Elijah Rock* as many times as necessary for singers to answer the first question. Multiple listenings may be needed. Discuss answers.
4. Listen to all of *Steal Away* and *Elijah Rock.* Answer Questions 2-4. Thoughtful multiple listenings may be needed.

Answers:

1. Discuss contrasts in tempo, dynamics, thickness of texture, overall emotional content.
2. Discuss similarities such as similar intensity of feelings, similar chord structures, similar textual subject matter.

3. and 4. Discuss personal responses to these open ended questions.

Global Folk Songs: Page 115

Lesson Objective:

The student is expected to compare and contrast the musical and emotional characteristics of folk songs from around the world.

National Standard 9A:

Students describe distinguishing characteristics of representative music genres and styles from a variety of cultures.

Materials:

 *¿Que Regalo?* from *Three Spanish Carols* arr. by Crocker (Spanish), *Listening CD*, Track 17

 *Sansa Kroma* arr. by Crocker (African), *Listening CD*, Track 18

 *S'vivon* arr. by Smith (Hebrew), *Listening CD*, Track 19

Directions:

1. Distribute copies of Global Folk Songs activity sheet.
2. Read and discuss the information presented.
3. Instruct the class to read the three questions on the worksheet in order to focus their attention on what to listen for in each folk song.
4. Play each global folk song for the class, asking students to listen for the two that are most similar. Multiple listenings may be needed.
5. Answer Question 1. Discuss answers.
6. Play each of the three global folk songs again to allow the class to select which two are the most different.
7. Answer Question 2. Discuss answers.
8. Play again only if students need aural cues to answer Questions 3-4.
9. Allow students time to look through their Essential Repertoire book to answer Question 5.
10. Extensions: Encourage students to search the internet to explore the music of the countries represented in the Global Folk Songs activity sheet.

Answers:

The answers to these questions are subjective in nature. Use student answers as a springboard for discussion rather than as a summative grading opportunity.

MUSIC ACROSS THE CURRICULUM

Reading Comprehension – Recognize Outcomes: Page 117

Musical Objective:
The student will examine how a song can take on many different meanings, texts, and interpretations.

Curricular Objective:
Reading Comprehension: The student will perceive relationships and recognize outcomes in a variety of written texts.

Materials:

Shenandoah arr. by Spevacek,
Listening CD, Track 20

Directions:
1. Distribute copies of Reading: Recognize Outcomes activity sheet.
2. Ask students to listen to *Shenandoah* while they are reading the words.
3. Read carefully the information section about the various meanings of *Shenandoah* before completing the worksheet.
4. Discuss the variety of answers among class members.

Answers:
Answers will vary. Accept any well-reasoned answer. These should be personal responses.

Reading Comprehension – Meaning & Supporting Ideas: Page 118

Musical Objective:
The student will identify the meaning of the text in order to perform the piece more musically.

Curricular Objective:
Reading Comprehension: The student will determine the meaning of words in a variety of written texts and identify supporting ideas in a variety of written texts.

Materials:

Sound the Trumpet by Purcell,
Listening CD, Track 21

Directions:
1. Distribute copies of Reading Comprehension: Meaning & Supporting Ideas activity sheet.
2. Read and discuss information presented.
3. Ask students to silently read the words to *Sound the Trumpet*. An alternative might be to read aloud and discuss the words.
4. Answer question Question 1 without listening to the recording.
5. Now play the recording of *Sound the Trumpet* and answer Questions 2 and 3.
6. Discuss the variety of responses.
7. Extension: Follow similar procedures using the text to the piece your choir is currently singing.

Answers:
1a. Mood is happy, joyful, celebrating an event
1b. Specific words might include: sprightly, shores rebound, instruments of joy, celebrate, glories;
2. Reasons vary; count any legitimate response as correct **3.** Non-religious (secular). It was written for Queen Mary's birthday. However, there is nothing in the text that indicates that "to celebrate the glories of this day" couldn't be a joyful religious celebration. Use the text for discussion. Count any well-reasoned response as correct.

Reading Comprehension – Relationships & Meaning of Words: Page 119

Musical Objective:
The student will analyze the meaning of the text in order to perform the piece more musically.

Curricular Objective:
Reading Comprehension: The student will determine the meaning of words in a variety of written texts. The student will perceive relationships and recognize outcomes in a variety of written texts.

Materials:

Turtle Dove arr. Spevacek,
Listening CD, Track 22

Directions:
1. Distribute copies of Reading Comprehension: Relationships & Meaning of Words activity sheet.
2. Silently read the words to *Turtle Dove.*
3. Answer question number 1-2 without listening to the recording.
4. Now listen to the recording of *Turtle Dove* and answer questions 3-4.
5. Discuss the variety of responses to the open-ended questions 3 and 4.
6. Extension: Follow similar procedures using the text to the piece your choir is currently singing.

Answers:
1. Fare means good wishes and good bye (fare well). Fair means pretty, attractive, beautiful **2.** Two is the most probable answer. Two lovers are discussing their love for each other **3. & 4.** Reasons vary, count any legitimate response as correct.

Note: Correct Question 4 as if it were a creative writing assignment. Discuss various answers. Discuss how the choir's performance of the song might be different depending upon the ending the group created.

Reading Comprehension – Inferences and Generalizations: Page 120

Musical Objective:
The student will analyze the meaning of the text in order to perform the song more musically.

Curricular Objective:
Reading Comprehension: The student will analyze information in a variety of written texts in order to make inferences and generalizations.

Materials:
Student copies of selected song to be analyzed.

Directions:
1. Select a song that has an interesting and meaningful text. It is particularly helpful to select a song that is currently being rehearsed.
2. Distribute copies of Reading Comprehension: Inferences and Generalizations activity sheet.
3. Read the directions and carefully follow all instructions.

Answer:
All questions are open-ended and depend on the particular song chosen. Accept all well-reasoned and well-supported answers.

Reading Comprehension – Meaning of Words: Page 121

Musical Objective:
The student will analyze the meaning of the text in order to perform the piece more musically.

Curricular Objective:
Reading Comprehension: The student will determine the meaning of words in a variety of written texts.

Materials:

Cripple Creek arr. Crocker,
Listening CD, Track 10

Directions:

1. Distribute copies of Reading Comprehension: Meaning of Words activity sheet.
2. Silently read the words to *Cripple Creek* as written on the worksheet as you listen to the recording of *Cripple Creek.*
3. Answer Questions 1-2. Play the recording as many times as necessary.

Answers:

1a. Cripple Creek might be in any part of America in which watermelons are grown **1b.** Various states are possible. Check where watermelons are grown. Check for the words Cripple Creek on a U.S. map. Discuss various answers and accept any well-reasoned response. **1c.** Probably teenagers **1d.** To see his girlfriend **1e.** Goin' in a run. Goin' in a whirl. Goes to see her in the middle of the week (not just on the weekend). **2.** What might Cripple Creek represent? Accept any answer which reasons that Cripple Creek might be any kind of a barrier (wall, objection of others, anything that keeps Johnny from getting what he wants). Accept all well-reasoned answers. Discuss the variety of answers.

Reading Comprehension – Summarize Text: Page 122

Musical Objective:

The student will examine the meaning of the text in order to perform a work more musically.

Curricular Objective:

Reading Comprehension: The student will summarize a variety of written texts.

Materials:

Student copies of selected song to be summarized.

Directions:

1. Select a meaningful text from one of the works your choir is rehearsing.
2. Distribute copies of Reading Comprehension: Summarize Text activity sheet.
3. Ask students to summarize the meaning of the text.
4. Discuss the variety of answers among class members.

Answers:

Answers will vary. Accept any well-reasoned answer.

Writing – Organize Ideas, Part 1: Page 123

Musical Objective:
The student will examine the mood of music based solely on listening.

Curricular Objective:
Written Communication: The student will organize ideas in a written composition on a given topic.

Materials:

Ju Me Leve un Bel Maitín ed. Goodale, *Listening CD*, Track 12

Directions:
1. Distribute copies of Writing: Organize Ideas on *Ju Me Leve un Bel Maitín*, Part I activity sheet.
2. Ask students to consider the question posed in the worksheet and compose an essay giving their opinions on that issue.
3. Discuss the variety of answers among class members.

Answers:
Answers will vary. Accept any well-reasoned answer. Hints: *Ju Me Leve un Bel Maitín* is secular, joyful, uplifting, playful.

Writing – Organize Ideas, Part 2: Page 124

Musical Objective:
The student will examine how text and music interrelate.

Curricular Objective:
Written Communication: The student will organize ideas in a written composition on a given topic.

Materials:

Ju Me Leve un Bel Maitín ed. Goodale, *Listening CD*, Track 12

Directions:
1. Distribute copies of Writing: Organize Ideas on *Ju Me Leve un Bel Maitín*, Part II activity sheet.
2. NOTE: Students must complete Part I before doing this activity (Part II).
3. Ask students to listen to the piece while they are reading the words. Did their opinions change after they read the translation? Was their original opinion of the meaning of the text valid after they read the text?
4. Discuss the variety of answers among class members.

Answers:
Answers will vary. Accept any well-reasoned answer. These should be personal responses.

Writing – Organize Ideas on Rhythm Errors: Page 125

Musical Objective:
The student will examine errors in music and consider how those errors relate to mistakes in rhythm.

Curricular Objective:
Written Communication: The student will organize ideas in a written composition on a given topic.

Directions:
1. Distribute copies of Writing: Organize Ideas on Rhythm Errors activity sheet.
2. Ask students to consider the posed question and compose an essay giving their opinions on that issue.
3. Discuss the variety of answers among class members.
4. Extension: View a copy of Robert Shaw conducting the Brahms *Requiem* or the Bach *B Minor Mass* in Carnegie Hall. These rehearsal videos (commercially available) demonstrate his ideas about rhythm errors as the root of most choral mistakes.

Answers:
Answers will vary. Accept any well-reasoned answer.

Writing – Organizing Ideas Evaluating Choral Performance Essay: Page 126

Musical Objective:
The student will evaluate a recent choral performance.

Curricular Objective:
Written Communication: The student will organize ideas in a written composition on a given topic.

Directions:
1. Distribute copies of Writing: Organizing Ideas: Evaluating Choral Performance activity sheet.
2. Carefully review the directions.
3. Create an essay based on your decisions as described in the worksheet.
4. Discuss the variety of answers among class members.

Answers:
Multiple answers are possible. Accept any well-reasoned answer.

Writing – Develop a Central Idea: Page 127

Musical Objective:
The student will examine the importance of fine arts in the school curriculum.

Curricular Objective:
Written Communication: The student will generate a written composition that develops/supports/elaborates the central idea stated in a given topic.

Directions:
1. Distribute copies of Writing: Develop a Central Idea activity sheet.
2. Ask students to carefully read the directions. Discuss the assignment to check for understanding.
3. After completing the essay, ask students to discuss the variety of answers among other class members.

Answers:
Answers will vary. Accept any well-reasoned answer. These should be personal responses.

Writing – Respond to a Given Audience: Page 128

Musical Objective:
The student will write an introduction to choral pieces appropriate for a specified audience.

Curricular Objective:
Written Communication: The student will respond appropriately in a written composition to the purpose/audience specified in a given topic.

Directions:
1. Distribute copies of Writing: Respond to a Given Audience activity sheet.
2. Carefully read the directions.
3. Create an essay based on your decisions as described in the worksheet.
4. Discuss the variety of answers among class members.

Answers:
Multiple answers are possible. Accept any well-reasoned answer.

Social Studies – History and Writing: Page 129

Musical Objective:
The student will compare and contrast two choral works from different time periods.

Curricular Objective:
Written Composition: The student will organize ideas in a written composition on a given topic.

Materials:

Sound the Trumpet by Purcell, *Listening CD*, Track 21

In Praise of Spring by Mendelsohn *Listening CD*, Track 6

Directions
1. Distribute copies of History & Writing activity sheet.
2. Carefully read the Background Information in the History & Writing activity sheet.
3. Listen to the recording of both the choral works listed.
4. Answer all questions. Multiple listenings will be necessary.
5. Discuss the variety of answers on Question 3 among class members.

Answers:
1. Important events
a. Purcell: Galileo identifies gravity; first English colony in America; Isaac Newton formulates principles of physics and math; Milton writes *Paradise Lost*; Rembrandt & Rubens are active painters, etc.
b. Mendelssohn: French Revolution, Lewis & Clark explore northwest; Metronome invented; First railroad; Morse invents telegraph, etc.
2. Similarities between the two compositions:
Both pieces are joyful, celebratory, at a fast tempo; use both polyphony and homophony; emphasize rhythm (definite beat present); use music to express a specific emotion, etc.
3. Speed of change today; Answers will vary. Accept any well-reasoned answer.

Social Studies – African-American Composers: Page 130

Musical Objective:
The student will examine the influence of African-American composers on the world of music.

Curricular Objective:
Written Communication: The student will generate a written composition that develops/supports/ elaborates the central idea stated in a given topic.

Directions:
1. Distribute copies of Social Studies: African-American Composers activity sheet.
2. Carefully review the directions.
3. Write answers to the questions posed.
4. Discuss the variety of answers among class members.

Answers:
African-American composers/performers: Select performers from jazz, popular music, rhythm & blues, etc. Classical composer suggestions are listed on the worksheet.

Most students will probably be able to generate a long list for Question 1. The length of these lists is one measure of the influence of African-Americans on the world of music.

Social Studies – Women Composers: Page 131

Musical Objective:
The student will compare and contrast women composers of the Twentieth Century with those of the Romantic Era.

Curricular Objective:
Written Communication: The student will generate a written composition that develops/supports/ elaborates the central idea stated in a given topic.

Directions:
1. Distribute copies of Women Composers worksheet and Historical Timelines (Romantic Era); and Historical Timeline (Twentieth Century).
2. Carefully read the directions in the Social Studies: Women Composers activity sheet
3. Write answers to the questions posed.
4. Discuss the variety of answers among class members.

Answers:
1. 4 **2.** None **3.** Why differences? Women had more children in Romantic time; Day care was not available; Women were not encouraged to be composers; Women were not all educated; Women DID compose, but historians just didn't write about them, etc; **4.** More opportunities exist for women composers today. Multiple answers are possible. Accept any well-reasoned answer.

Social Studies – Hispanic Composers: Page 132

Musical Objective:
The student will examine the influence of Hispanic composers on the world of music.

Curricular Objective:
Written Communication: The student will generate a written composition that develops/supports/ elaborates the central idea stated in a given topic.

Directions:
1. Distribute copies of Social Studies: Hispanic Composers activity sheet.
2. Carefully review the directions.
3. Write answers to the questions posed.
4. Discuss the variety of answers among class members.

Answers:
Hispanic composers/performers: Select performers from a wide variety of mediums. Classical composer suggestions are listed in Question No. 4.

Most students will probably be able to generate a long list for Question 1. The length of these lists is one measure of the influence of Hispanic music on the world of music.

Social Studies – Global Folk Songs: Page 133

Musical Objective:
The student will compare and contrast folk songs from around the world.

Curricular Objective:
Written Communication: The student will organize ideas in a written composition on a given topic.

Materials:

Elijah Rock arr. Hogan
Listening CD, Track 16

Ju Me Leve un Bel Maitín arr. Goodale
Listening CD, Track 12

¿A Que Regalo? arr. Crocker
Listening CD, Track 17

Sansa Kroma arr. Crocker
Listening CD, Track 18

S'vivon arr. Smith
Listening CD, Track 19

Directions:
1. Distribute copies of Global Folk Songs activity sheet.
2. Carefully read the Background Information.
3. Listen to the recording of each of the five global folk songs.
4. Select one of the folk songs to emphasize. Consider and write an essay about that song.
5. Encourage students to research additional information about their chosen country.

Answers:
Answers will vary depending on the folk song selected. Accept any well-reasoned answers.

Mathematics – Bar Graphs: Page 134 Analyzing a Bar Graph: Page 135

Musical Objective:
The student will analyze potential balance problems within a choir by analyzing the differing sizes of the various voice parts.

Curricular Objective:
Mathematics – Concepts: The student will demonstrate an understanding of measurement concepts using metric and customary units.

Directions:
- If you have not already done so, divide singers into sections (soprano, alto, tenor, bass, etc.).
- Distribute copies of Bar Graphs or Analyzing a Bar Graph activity sheets.
- Follow directions carefully.
- Complete the worksheet as directed.
- Discuss answers.

Answers:
Page 134 Bar Graphs
1. Draw bar graph showing number of singers on each part. Answers will vary.

Page 135 Analyzing a Bar Graph
1. Total number in choir
2. Total number on one voice part
3. Divide total number on one voice part by total number in choir to get the percentage
4. Answers will vary.
5. Balance refers to the loudness or softness of individual sections as compared to the other sections of the choir.

6.-7. Open-ended questions. Should be counted as correct if the answer is reasonable. Multiple correct answers are possible. Discuss the variety of answers that the class gave.

Mathematics – Problem Solving: Page 136

Musical Objective:
The student will analyze potential profit margins for selling commemorative CDs.

Curricular Objective:
Mathematics – Problem Solving: The student will determine solution strategies and will analyze or solve problems.

Directions:
1. Distribute copies of Mathematics: Problem Solving activity sheet.
2. Read the directions printed on the top of the worksheet, and carefully follow all instructions.
3. Compute answers for items a-d and chart at bottom of page.
4. Discuss and compare answers.

Answers:
1. $5100 **2.** 340 **3.** 368 **4.** $5.10
5. Open-ended answer. Discussion of different ideas and opinions.

6. Based on 1000 CDs:
a. $5100 **b.** 340 **c.** 368 **d.** $5.10

Based on 2000 CDs:
a. $5950 **b.** 397 **c.** 383 **d.** $2.98

Based on 500 CDs:
a. $4675 **b.** 312 **c.** 361 **d.** $9.35